i and
ights.

Discovery and Invention

Discovery and Invention

The Urban Plays of Lanford Wilson

Anne M. Dean

Rutherford ● Madison ● Teaneck
Fairleigh Dickinson University Press
London and Toronto: Associated University Presses

Associated University Presses
440 Forsgate Drive
Cranbury, NJ 08512

Associated University Presses
25 Sicilian Avenue
London WC1A 2QH, England

Associated University Presses
P.O. Box 338, Port Credit
Mississauga, Ontario
Canada L5G 4L8

The paper used in this publication meets the requirements
of the American National Standard for Permanence of Paper
for Printed Library Materials Z39.48-1984.

Library of Congress Cataloging-in-Publication Data

Dean, Anne, 1950–
  Discovery and invention : the urban plays of Lanford Wilson / Anne
M. Dean.
    p.   cm.
  Includes bibliographical references and index.
  ISBN 0-8386-3548-2 (alk. paper)
  1. Wilson, Lanford, 1937–   —Criticism and interpretation.
  2. City and town life in literature.   I. Title.
  PS3573.I458Z63   1994
  812'.54—dc20   94-3180
                                                         CIP

For my darling mother:

And now good morrow to our waking soules
Which watch not one another out of feare;
For love, all love of other sights controules,
And makes one little roome, an every where.

(from The Good Morrow
by John Donne)

and for my Godchildren:

Ben, Laurence, and Madeline

Contents

Preface   9
Acknowledgments   11

1. From Missouri to Manhattan   15
2. Concerns, Poetry, and Dramatized Experience   30
3. *Balm in Gilead*   61
4. *The Hot l Baltimore*   80
5. *Burn This*   94
6. Conclusion   123

Notes   125
Bibliography   134
Index   137

Preface

To attempt a totally exhaustive study of Lanford Wilson's work since the beginning of what has been an astonishingly prolific career would have been a gargantuan task, and there would have been scarcely room to offer any criticism or analysis of each play mentioned. Selection has therefore been inevitable; my main problem was to select those works that I believe best illustrate Wilson's achievement as a dramatist and that include first-rate examples of his superb facility with language.

After much consideration, I decided to concentrate upon his three major "city" plays. Chronologically, these are: *Balm in Gilead* (1964), *The Hotl Baltimore* (1973) and *Burn This* (1987). Since Wilson is perhaps best known for plays depicting rural and small-town life such as *The Rimers of Eldritch*, *This Is the Rill Speaking* and the Pulitzer prize–winning *Talley's Folly*, this decision may at first seem to be rather perverse; it is, however, my belief that the intensity, authenticity, and sheer dramatic scope of his urban drama most clearly demonstrate the extent of his abilities as a dramatic poet.

Spanning three decades, these plays not only show Wilson at his very best, but also cover crucial periods in his development as a writer. His early experimental work on Off-Off Broadway revealed Wilson as a talent to watch, his acute sense of timing and original use of language already resoundingly in evidence. With admirable economy, he could mold character and define subtle linguistic personalities, at the same time imbuing his work with what has been described as poetic realism—the means by which he contrives to turn even the most ordinary speech into emotionally translucent poetry.

Balm in Gilead is acknowledged as one of the most influential plays of its day; simultaneously surreal and naturalistic, it achieves with great accuracy and compassion a stylized evocation of the lives of a group of drug addicts, prostitutes, and hustlers whose raw utterances and often deranged monologues convey the essence of their predicament. Ten years later, Wilson had moved away from the tricks and *coups de théâtre* of his early drama and was now accepted as a more conventional—though often surprising—playwright, in the tradition of writers like Tennessee Williams.

With its theme of decay and loss, of unfulfilled dreams and romantic longing, *The Hotl Baltimore* is, in some ways Wilson's *A Streetcar Named Desire*. It is also a refinement of the discordant music he found in *Balm in Gilead;* the poetry of language is now completely integrated and unselfconscious, and arises quite naturally out of the action.

During the next decade, Wilson's drama became increasingly sophisticated. Adapting and building upon the techniques utilised in his earlier work, he continued to seek new ways of presenting poetic, yet realistic language onstage. This reached its apotheosis in *Burn This;* here, Wilson creates an amalgamation of the kind of impoverished and debased language he used in *Balm in Gilead* with the cultured, literate tones of artistic mid-Manhattan in order to explore, among other things, the nature of creative art and the personal price that must be paid in order to achieve it. *Burn This* encompasses themes that have marbled Wilson's work from the outset, and is a perfect example of the maturity and depth he has attained.

Although this book concentrates primarily upon Wilson's urban plays, I have included pertinent references to much of his other work in order to set them in context. For similar reasons,I have incorporated a chapter giving biographical information; in this way, one can more easily chart Wilson's progress as a young, enthusiastic playwright from the early 1960s toward his position as one of the most respected dramatists currently working in the United States.

Also included are extracts from interviews conducted with Wilson himself, with Marshall Mason, who has to date directed forty-two productions of twenty-three of his plays, with Tanya Berezin, Artistic Director of the Circle Repertory Company in New York, where Wilson is Playwright in Residence, with Michael Warren Powell, long-time associate of Wilson and actor in a number of his early plays, and with the entire cast and director of the 1990 London production of *Burn This.*

Acknowledgments

I am indebted to Lanford Wilson for agreeing to be interviewed during my visit to New York to research this book, and for his kindness, encouragement, and permission to use extracts from his plays. I was also fortunate enough to interview some of Mr. Wilson's closest colleagues: Tanya Berezin, Marshall Mason, and Michael Warren Powell. The extent of their courtesy and the invaluable insights provided cannot be overstated. This visit would not have been possible without a generous grant from The Society of Authors, to whom I also extend my gratitude and appreciation.

I must also thank the director and cast of the 1990 London production of *Burn This,* interviewed in the course of research, both for their kindness and excellent contributions: Robert Allan Ackerman, Lou Liberatore, John Malkovich, Michael Simkins, and Juliet Stevenson. My thanks also to BBC Television for their permission to use excerpts from interviews included in their *Omnibus* program on John Malkovich, and to the *New York Times* for allowing me to include extracts from various articles on Mr. Wilson's work.

Researching and writing works such as this would be a singularly less enjoyable experience without the unceasing support and discerning, intelligent analysis offered by Irene Kemp; to her, I extend my warmest thanks for all her help. Special thanks, too, to Sally Maseyk for her assistance and encouragement and, indeed, to all of my friends. Finally, may I express my incalculable appreciation to my parents, who have supported and helped me every step of the way.

Discovery and Invention

1

From Missouri to Manhattan

Lanford Eugene Wilson was born in Lebanon, Missouri on 13
April 1937, the only child of Ralph and Violetta Wilson, who
divorced when he was five. Wilson lived with his mother and
grandmother in various locations around Missouri throughout
his childhood and adolescence; despite being "poor, very poor,"[1]
this was a happy time and Wilson recalls it with affection. Wilson
is now in close contact with both sides of his family, maintaining
"very special feelings"[2] toward them.

Although Wilson enjoyed a happy childhood with his maternal
guardians, the early dislocation in his family life affected him
deeply, and echoes of this deep influence can be found in the
majority of his work. Time and again, he portrays people without
a firm home base, or who in some way feel apart from the rest of
society; his compassionate depiction of such "outsiders" constitutes one of the most notable features of his drama.

Similarly, the disruption almost certainly contributed to his frequent dramatization of family groups, whether in the form of
traditional relationships or, more often, of an unconventional,
even controversial, nature. Surrogate families abound in Wilson's
work from his earliest plays to his latest. One of the more extreme
examples occurs in *Balm in Gilead,* where he depicts individuals
who exist on the very edge of society. These lonely and deracinated people combine to form a family of sorts, no matter how
unsatisfactory. They cling together for solace and support, seeking affection even in the most tawdry relationships.

Wilson enjoyed school and, besides his love of track sports, developed a keen interest in art and film; this led to frequent forays
to local cinemas where he devoured all he saw. These visits fired
his enthusiasm for acting and prompted him to become involved
in school plays. He subsequently performed in a number of high-

school productions, most notably as Tom in Tennessee Williams's *The Glass Menagerie*. Productions of Arthur Miller's *Death of a Salesman* and, especially, a travelling roadshow production of *Brigadoon* consolidated his interest in the potential of the theatre; Wilson found this show absolutely spellbinding, and recalls how "after that town came back to life on stage, movies didn't stand a chance."[3] Despite his youthful enthusiasm, a number of years would pass before he considered playwriting as a possible career; for a boy in a small Midwestern town, such a notion must have seemed utterly fantastic and unattainable.

After high school Wilson attended Southwest Missouri State College, but left without obtaining his degree. These were uncertain times, and Wilson had little idea about the direction his future might take. He was interested in art, but also enjoyed short story writing, though the latter was at the time more a hobby than a possible career, and not therefore really taken very seriously.

With a view to reclaiming at least some of the time he had been deprived of paternal guidance, he decided to move to San Diego to live with his father, whom he had not seen for thirteen years. Here, he worked as a riveter in the Ryan Aircraft Plant, as well as spending a year at the State College, where he studied art and art history. As a result, Wilson considered that he might become an artist or a specialist in graphic design. This period was, however, both traumatic and unhappy. The reunion with his father was disastrous; the two men disagreed on many issues, and Wilson felt both rejected and frustrated. The effect upon him was profound and, a number of years later, Wilson attempted to exorcize some of the pain he felt through a dramatization of these events. The result was *Lemon Sky*, a highly emotional autobiographical work dealing with the confrontation of two men with few ideas in common.

Following the débâcle of this doomed reunion, Wilson moved to Chicago, where he lived for the next six years. The culture shock he experienced upon living for the first time in a huge, industrialized city was immense; he found the pressure exciting, but for a while he struggled to survive, taking on any odd jobs that became available.

Attracted to the freedom of an unconventional, even bohemian lifestyle, he became involved in the counterculture of the city, sharing late-night café tables with the kind of people he would later

portray in works such as *Balm in Gilead* and *The Hotl Baltimore*.
For a while, he also worked as a male prostitute, becoming even
more familiar with the underside of urban life. He confirmed this
to Don Shewey, readily and candidly admitting his involvement:
"Sure. How am I supposed to know about all this? . . . Certainly
in Chicago and the first two years in New York. Through an
agency."[4] Although he was probably unaware of it at the time,
Wilson was also collating first-rate raw material for his drama.
"You get some fun lines,"[5] he now says of his days as a hustler.

Wilson eventually obtained a post as a graphic artist in an advertising agency, but this occupation was not to hold his interest for
very long. He knew he wanted to work in the arts, but was unsure
whether graphic design was the route to take. Throughout the
hectic period prior to his employment at the agency, and outside
of working hours, he had continued to write short stories, thoroughly enjoying this activity since it focused his literary imagination and channelled his creative energies.

Upon rereading one such story, Wilson suddenly considered
the possibility that it might work better as a play—something he
had never attempted before. He recalls that, before he had even
completed the first page, he "knew [he] was a playwright."[6] After
revising the whole story, he was so excited with the result—although with hindsight he has stated that his effort was "rotten"[7]—
that he decided there and then that playwriting was where his
destiny lay.

Thus, the inexperienced, though determined, Wilson enrolled
at a playwriting class at the University of Chicago, where he wrote
numerous one-act plays. Heavily influenced by the writing of Tennessee Williams and Eugene O'Neill, he recalls an early play, *The
Hour Glass,* as resembling "an O'Neill sea story as if it were written
by Tennessee Williams."[8] Indeed, he believes that all of his early
efforts were totally unproduceable, although in later years he was
to loot successfully these early works for plots and characters.

In the summer of 1962, Wilson moved to New York's Greenwich
Village with a view to finding a foothold in the vibrant theatre
scene there. During these busy, experimental days, Wilson supported himself—while accumulating a mass of potential dramatic
material—by working in the complaints department of a furni-
ture company, as a waiter, and as a hotel reservations clerk. He
eventually found a job in the subscriptions office of the New York

Shakespeare Festival, and his proximity to the realities of a life in the theatre only increased his desire to be an active participant.

The turning point came during a casual visit to the Caffe Cino, an Off-Off Broadway venue in Greenwich Village that was showing Eugene Ionesco's *The Lesson*. Wilson recalls the experience as being supremely important to him, showing him that "theater could be dangerous and funny in that way at the same time."[9] But the significance of the evening did not end there; after the show, he met the producer, Joseph Cino, one of the cofounders with Ellen Stewart of the Off-Off Broadway movement. From that moment there was no turning back. Cino had been instrumental in establishing Off-Off Broadway as a viable alternative to many Off-Broadway theatres, which had declined due to burgeoning financial constraints into a level of commercialism almost—but not quite—on a par with mainstream Broadway.

With indefatigable enthusiasm and confidence in the value of the new writers they encouraged, Cino and Stewart began mounting controversial and challenging productions in the Caffe Cino and the La Mama Experimental Theatre Club. The atmosphere in these venues was informal but stimulating, and the careers of many unorthodox young dramatists began there: Sam Shepard, David Rabe, John Guare, and Wilson himself, to name but a few.

Wilson had been waiting for an opportunity like this; at last, he had found an interested and encouraging mentor who would not only read and critique his work, but would also give it a production. Cino encouraged Wilson to submit a script for production at the Caffe, and Wilson was delighted to accept the invitation; he had by this time amassed an enormous collection of finished— and unfinished—material, and the first of his plays to be seen Off-Off Broadway was *So Long at the Fair*. With obvious irony, Wilson describes the work as being a "silly comedy"[10] about a boy from the Midwest who "failed at every single art he has tried."[11] However, this modest deprecation ceased to bear any truth following the play's successful premiere at the Caffe in August 1963.

So Long at the Fair was followed in 1964 by a double-bill of *No Trespassing* and *Home Free!*, again at the Caffe. The latter attracted considerable critical acclaim, which eventually led to its transfer to the Cherry Lane Theatre, Off-Broadway, on a triple-bill with new works by Sam Shepard and Paul Foster, who were then considered to be the most promising new dramatists; the sponsor was veteran playwright, Edward Albee. This transfer was not only auspicious as Wilson's first real taste of success, but it also introduced him to director Marshall Mason, with whom he would later found (along with Tanya Berezin and Rob Thirkield) the Circle Repertory Company in New York.

Wilson followed *Home Free!* with *The Madness of Lady Bright*, another short play, again premiered by Joe Cino, which has also been seen and well received in London and Paris. During 1964, he completed *Balm in Gilead,* his first full-length drama. The work was produced by Ellen Stewart in January 1965 at the La Mama Experimental Theatre Club in New York. Two subsequent revivals have taken place, both directed by John Malkovich; the first was presented by the Steppenwolf Theatre Ensemble at the Steppenwolf Theatre in Chicago in September 1980, and the second was a joint production by the Circle Repertory Company and Steppenwolf, staged at the Circle Repertory Theatre in New York in May 1984. Critical response to *Balm in Gilead* was largely favorable, the *Village Voice* describing it as a brilliant piece of work that was "basically documentary."[12] In the same year, *Ludlow Fair,* another one-act play, was produced, again at the Caffe Cino.

During 1965, Wilson wrote several plays, all of which were premiered either at the Caffe Cino or at the La Mama Repertory Theatre: *This Is the Rill Speaking* (which he also directed and which was subsequently taken on a tour of Europe and, in 1967, performed as part of a dramatic arts educational series on American television); *The Sand Castle; Miss Williams: A Turn; Days Ahead* and *Sex Is Between Two People.* During 1966, *Wandering: A Turn* was produced, as well as another full-length work, *The Rimers of Eldritch,* which won Wilson the Drama Desk Vernon Rice Award for best Off-Off Broadway achievement of 1967. During 1967, Wilson was awarded a Rockefeller Foundation Grant (he was to receive a further Grant in 1973). In the same year, *Home Free!* and *The Madness of Lady Bright* were both performed—to great acclaim—at the Mercury Theatre in London by a group calling themselves the American Theatre Project; several members of this group would, only two years later, form the Circle Repertory Company in New York.

In such a fecund atmosphere, the art of improvisation came into its own; theatre workers involved in these experimental productions were usually young, fresh, innovative and thirsty for new experiences. Wilson and his colleagues shared everything, and thrived on each other's intoxicating enthusiasm and invention. Wilson recalls the sheer excitement of such times:

> I can't believe the energy we had then. . . . It was all very intense and exciting. There was a kind of independent collective Off-Off Broadway: if one of us discovered something, it belonged to everyone. We were all . . . so strongly what we were. I felt like we were what the Impressionists must have been.[13]

This sense of euphoria was, however, to be short-lived. In 1967, Joe Cino committed suicide. For Wilson, this was a devastating blow. It was more than the death of a revered colleague, it was akin to losing the affection and support of a father for the second time in his life. The two men had formed a profound and trusting relationship, with Wilson transferring his once-thwarted emotions to this new surrogate father. Wilson recalls:

> All he [Cino] ever wanted for himself was enough money to keep the Caffe Cino going. . . . On nights when nobody came to see the play, we'd put it on just for Joe. . . . When your father and boss and preacher kills himself, you find yourself without much to believe in. Everyone—except Joe—knew that he was creating a new theatre in America. His excitement was responsible for half of the vitality of Off-Off Broadway, and his death heralded the end of free activity. After Joe died, Off-Off Broadway got less communal, more competitive.[14]

Lacking the security and support of the production "company" that Caffe Cino and The La Mama Experimental Theatre Club had become, Wilson began to search for new venues for his work and, in the early days, could only offer plays he had already written. Several had been completed during 1967 and, in 1968, *Untitled Play, The Gingham Dog,* and *Lemon Sky* received their premieres at the Judson Poets' Theatre in New York, the Washington Theatre Club in Washington D.C., and the Eugene O'Neill Memorial Theatre in Waterford, Connecticut, respectively. Additionally, in 1968, Wilson received an ABC-Yale Fellowship.

Although the Washington production of *The Gingham Dog* received considerable critical acclaim, with Richard L. Coe of the Washington Post describing it as "a work of clear and substantial value,"[15] when it transferred to Broadway, it closed after only five performances. Thus ended Wilson's first taste of Broadway. Such brevity of exposure was typical of Broadway during the 1960s and 1970s, when commercialism dominated the theatrical scene; the production of ever more extravagant musicals with famous star names in the casts formed the staple theatrical diet. As a result of this prevailing mood, the success of a serious play became a remarkable rarity. Wilson was disappointed in the play's apparent failure; it would be another ten years before he would have any success on Broadway. However, in many ways he prefers his work to be seen away from the Broadway arena, as he told Barnet Kellman in 1978:

> We *want* our plays done Off-Off Broadway. Very often I do, anyway. I guess a lot of us have had that Broadway thing, and know it's just impossible.[16]

Lemon Sky closed after only seventeen performances, but subsequently moved to Chicago, where it enjoyed a moderately successful run. In this work, Wilson reverted to some of the technical experiments of his earlier plays: aiming for a complex collage of effects, he counterpointed time lapses, upset the chronology of the piece, and utilized direct contact with the audience by having characters speak out into the stalls. John J. O'Connor in the *Wall Street Journal* remarked on Wilson's "extraordinary use of language,"[17] and Clive Barnes designated the work as "his best play so far."[18]

Despite the critical acclaim he received, this period was one of the unhappiest in Wilson's life, both professionally and emotionally. *Lemon Sky* was the last work that he would write for over eighteen months; the combination of Cino's death and the generally poor notices he had received for his last few plays had taken their toll. Wilson remembers that

> I had an incredible block after *Lemon Sky*. Maybe it was because I had grown up at the Cino, a theatre of participation, but I found that I just couldn't adapt to being a closet writer, to giving my play to a producer and waiting for the readings.[19]

During this period, Wilson again met Marshall Mason, who had directed *Home Free!* at the Cherry Lane Theatre some years before and, in 1969, the Circle Repertory Company was established—a true landmark in Wilson's life. Because the Company has played such an enormous part in Wilson's development as a playwright, it is worth looking at its origins and philosophy.

Wilson is, along with Mason, Tanya Berezin, and Rob Thirkield, one of the founding members of the Company and has been, since its inception in 1969, their premier Playwright in Residence—what Artistic Director Tanya Berezin describes as their "national treasure."[20] The Company evolved out of a cultural organization named Circle (from which they would later take their name). Its founders were much involved in the Off-Off Broadway movement of the early 1960s; all had worked together at one point or another during this period. Tanya Berezin's first involvement with Wilson had occurred when she appeared in the original production of *The Rimers of Eldritch* at Joe Cino's La Mama Experimental Theatre Club; she later worked with him again at the Caffe Cino on a revival of *This Is the Rill Speaking.*

Although not a founding member, Michael Warren Powell, a friend of Wilson's and the first actor to play Dopey in *Balm in Gilead,* also became involved with and undertook several projects with the group. In 1967, building on the contacts that Powell and Thirkield had established during their involvement with the La Mama Troupe on its tour of Europe in 1966, the group set out for London under the name of the American Theater Project. They performed Wilson's *Home Free!* and *The Madness of Lady Bright* at the Mercury Theatre in Notting Hill Gate to great acclaim. The group was much heartened by their success, but another two years would pass until they considered that they had accumulated sufficient expertise and professionalism to establish the Circle Repertory Company.

As a result of the writer's block he suffered for a period of eighteen months (which coincided with his early days with the Company) Wilson accumulated an excellent understanding of the theatrical arts. He took advantage of his literary stasis to immerse himself in the activities of the Company, at the same time observing and learning from everything around him. He helped with productions in any way he could, including moving props, becoming involved in set design, even acting. (He was a notable success in e.e. Cummings's *Him,* which left him an "absolute wreck,"[21] but in which he had "at least two evenings when he was really superb."[22]) Tanya Berezin notes:

> During the first year and a half, Lanford's main participation in the Company was to come to all of the workshops, all the rehearsals and performances and just stand there and watch. And learn about actors and the directors and everything that went on. . . . He has a very special sensitivity toward what it takes to do the other arts in the theatre and, as a result, when he writes he challenges actors and designers in really exciting ways.[23]

The *raison d'être* of the Circle Repertory Company was—and is—to encourage and develop new writing for the theatre, as well as to produce revivals of classic plays. Additionally, it is their intention to establish an ongoing ensemble of artists—including directors, actors, writers, technicians, and designers—who will pool their expertise to create an ever-evolving and developmental theatre.

Berezin describes the ambience of the Company as "very much a community of artists"[24] and believes that their early intentions of establishing an organic and creative organization have borne fruition:

> We had in mind a theatre company that responded to the needs of the artist; this philosophy is firmly ensconsed in the life of the Company, which means it is almost completely artist driven. This does not mean that it is politicized by votes or readings or whatever, but we all work very closely together and respect each other's input.[25]

Circle Repertory's intention is "to make the action of the play become the experience of the audience"[26]—a phrase originally coined by Marshall Mason. Berezin elaborates:

> We try to bring the audience into the play, not to objectify it in any kind of way—we're not attracted to presentational kinds of work—but to make it their experience. For me—and I think the other members of the Company—the excitement of theatre is that it is in the present moment, it's so ephemeral; when it's over, it's gone, it doesn't exist and it may never exist again. To have the audience experience that kind of vitality and to respond to it is what is important to me. We live together for two-and-a-half hours.[27]

It is one of the practices of the Company that the playwright is usually present right through the rehearsal process; here, no play is ever 'frozen,' and many have been revised even after the work has officially opened. Because of its experimental nature, the Company adopts a very flexible method of working, one aspect of which is the process known as a PIP—Project in Progress. Members of the Company organize a series of readings for new plays (they maintain a tradition of reading one new play every Friday afternoon), which are given their first exposure to assembled Company members such as actors, lighting technicians, and so on. The group then, as actor Lou Liberatore puts it, "tries to critique the work for the writer."[28] After the first readthrough of the play, two rough performances are given to a group of subscribers; actors perform, script in hand. Once the work has been 'approved,' it goes forward into production and, during this period, it is frequently revised still further.

This is clearly an extraordinarily creative method of working and has been used on several occasions with Wilson's work. However, Tanya Berezin believes that the most constructive method of developing Wilson's plays is to mount an initial production outside of New York, monitor its audience's response, and then clarify it as it evolves toward its Manhattan debut—invariably at the Company's playhouse, the tiny Circle Theatre on Sixth Avenue that was built out of an old garage. Wilson believes that his successful alliance with the Company is due to the following factors:

> There is a group of six or seven of us who trust each other. We know we're after the same thing, and we all know what that thing is and we have open discussion amongst ourselves. . . . the working conditions in the workshop we . . . feel produce the best poetry being written for the American stage.[29]

The work of the Company was greatly admired by Harold Clurman, one of the founders in the 1930s of The Group Theatre, a similarly rich melting pot for dramatic innovation that included the likes of Sanford Meisner and Clifford Odets:

> [The Circle Repertory Company] possesses a character of its own, an identity or "face," related to a particular place in the community. . . .
> In the ensemble or "team" of the Circle Theatre there is genuine

communication between actor and actor: they live in the same world, they are integral with their environment and are expressive of it.[30]

He goes on to note how actors

must be chosen from among people who share kindred ideals, training and emotional or intellectual background. And they have to stay together long enough to acquire a spontaneous sense of one another.[31]

One of the Company's leading actors, William Hurt, corroborates this, observing that

Our enthusiasm is alive here. It's like coming home. . . . Here, well, we care about the work. We don't have to go to the party, we don't need the limousine. All we need is enough to eat, and the work, and the mutual respect that comes from just being allowed to do that work.[32]

The founding of Circle Repertory was the beginning of a long and exceptionally fruitful relationship between Wilson and director Marshall Mason. Of the alliance between the two men, Tanya Berezin observes that

It is a wonderful relationship; their sensibility is so much alike. Lanford buries his plays, challenges you to find out what he is talking about, to find out what is happening, and Marshall has an amazing ability to pull out the meaning and clarify it without ironing it, without taking out the creases. Over the years, they have grown to respect each other's providence; Lanford is never threatened by Marshall's leaps because he understands what he means, and Marshall knows exactly what Lanford wants to convey. The other ingredient to their relationship is simply magic.[33]

Similarly, Mason states that

Lanford and I share the same vision of theater. . . . We are both interested in plays and acting that depict reality in all its depth and mystery and wonder and that do that in a kind of elevated way that allows some poetry, both in language and in visual stage imagery. The two of us share the same ideas about how to accomplish this.[34]

While Wilson's work is central to the company, a number of other playwrights are also heavily involved: Patrick Meyers, Edward J. Moore, Terence McNally, Milan Stitt, and Julie Bovasso, to name but a few. Work by those not directly associated with the group is also occasionally produced and the premieres of plays by writers like Jules Feiffer, Albert Innaurato, and Mark Medoff have been mounted. As Peter Buckley observes:

> As the only institutional theater in the country with playwrights in residence creating for specific actors, [the Company] is somewhat of a national resource in nourishing the repertories of theaters across the country.[35]

As the reputation of Circle Repertory has grown, so too has the level of support it receives. Donations have been received from celebrities such as Al Pacino, Stephen Sondheim, and Jack Lemmon, as well as from Joseph Papp of the New York Shakespeare Festival, whose support was the more remarkable since his organization was considered the Company's main Off-Broadway rival.

Toward the end of 1969, Wilson's one-act play *Stoop* was televised as part of New York television's prestigious "Theatre in America" series on PBS; in April 1970, while the Company was still struggling to survive, his *Serenading Louie* was produced at the Washington Theatre Club. It deals with murder and suicide, and its negative, even depressing effect upon audiences forced Wilson to review his pessimistic playwriting strategy. He "decided [he] didn't want to do that to an audience."[36] During this period, Wilson received the first of two Guggenheim Fellowships (the second was awarded in 1972).

Serenading Louie was followed in 1971 by the premiere of *Sextet (Yes)*, at the Circle Repertory Theatre, marking Wilson's first production with the Company. A year later Wilson wrote *The Great Nebula in Orion*, which was actually first staged at the Stables Theatre Club in Manchester, England, and later became the second of Wilson's plays to be staged by the Circle Repertory Company. The following year proved far happier for Wilson; he collaborated with one of his literary heroes, Tennessee Williams, on the libretto for Lee Hoiby's opera of *Summer and Smoke*.

Wilson followed his collaboration with Williams with *Ikke, Ikke, Nye, Nye, Nye,* staged at the Yale Cabaret in New Haven, Connecti-

cut. This was the last of his works not to be premiered at the
Circle Repertory Theatre. In May of the same year, *The Family
Continues* was also produced there.

1973 was, both artistically and critically, Wilson's most successful
year to date. During 1972, Marshall Mason had encouraged Wilson to write another full-length play, and the result was *The Hotl
Baltimore,* produced in 1973 and again directed by Mason. The
image of urban decay encapsulated in the play was one Wilson
had contemplated for some time; through the central image of
a condemned hotel in the once beautiful city of Baltimore, he
symbolized the inexorable deterioration of America.

With this play, Wilson put the Circle Repertory Company on
the map of international theatre; their reputation as a Company
of rare professionalism and innovation was firmly established and,
with growing support from various quarters, their future was
guaranteed. Virtually every member of the cast was singled out
for praise, and the play was hugely popular with audiences and
critics alike. After playing to packed houses at the Circle Repertory Theatre, it moved to the Circle in the Square Theatre in
Greenwich Village where it set a new Off-Broadway record with
1,166 performances. It was subsequently bought by ABC Television for a short series of situation comedies based around its
characters. The play won the following awards: the New York
Drama Critics Circle Award for Best American Play of 1972–73,
an Obie for the best Off-Broadway play, the Outer Circle Award,
and the John Gassner Playwriting Award. In 1974, Wilson received the American Institute of Arts and Letters Award for his
contribution to contemporary drama. *The Hotl Baltimore* was also
included in the Burns Mantle/Guernsey *Ten Best American Plays*
volume for that season.

The Mound Builders, written in 1975, won Wilson another Obie
award for Outstanding Playwright and, in 1976, the Circle Repertory production was subsequently used as part of the "Theatre in
America" series on PBS. This was followed in 1977 by *Brontosaurus,* and in 1978 by *5th of July,* later revised and renamed *Fifth of
July.* This work was the first of what is sometimes referred to as
Wilson's only trilogy, the so-called "War in Lebanon" plays, although Wilson does not regard them as forming any such pattern.
The remaining plays in this "series" are *Talley's Folly,* which won
the Pulitzer Prize in 1980, and *A Tale Told,* produced in 1981. This

play was later revised and retitled *Talley and Son,* which version had its first production in 1985.

In 1981, *Thymus Vulgaris* was premiered at the Lee Strasberg Institute in Los Angeles, and 1982 saw the first production of *Angels Fall,* a work in which a nuclear accident brings together a diverse group of individuals. This work was staged as part of the New World Festival in Miami, and was largely successful with the critics. For Frank Rich, the play was another fine example of Wilson's compassionate regard for those he dramatized: Rich noticed

> Wilson's talent for finding the humanity in everyone he places on a stage, whether the setting be the Hotel Baltimore or the Talley family's Missouri farm. . . . Mr. Wilson is one of the few artists in our theater who can truly make America sing.[37]

This was followed in 1986 by *A Bethrothal* at the Man in the Moon Theatre in London.

The first production of *Burn This,* which Wilson had been commissioned to write by the Circle Repertory Company, was presented at the Mark Taper Forum in Los Angeles in 1987, directed by Marshall Mason. It would prove to be the last play he directed before leaving the Company, and it is fitting that his departure, like the group's inception, should be marked by his close involvement with Wilson.

Following its premiere in California, Circle Repertory took the play to New York, where it played at the 890 Theatre. Later the same year, the Steppenwolf Theatre Company produced the work at the Royal George Theatre in Chicago. It opened on Broadway at the Plymouth Theatre in October 1987. Although it was initially received rather coolly in the United States, attracting a tepid and unenthusiastic response from the crucial *New York Times,* the play nevertheless completed a fairly successful run. John Malkovich recalls how "it was the first time in fifteen years that a straight play had run with a lukewarm review."[38]

In 1990, *Burn This* transferred to London for a sell-out run at the Hampstead Theatre. Such was the enthusiasm for the play that long lines for returned tickets began forming and, before long, the show was being hailed as essential viewing. At the end of its fringe run, it transferred to even more acclaim to the Lyric

Theatre in Shaftesbury Avenue, where again it played to constantly full houses.

During 1991, Wilson was engaged in completing *Redwood Curtain* which premiered in New York during 1992.

Wilson remains closely involved with the Playwrights Laboratory at the Circle Repertory Company, frequently attending readings and rehearsals and offering advice and guidance to its predominantly young membership. There is no reason to believe that this always prolific writer will not continue to produce complex and exciting drama for a very long time to come.

2

Concerns, Poetry, and Dramatized Experience

Lanford Wilson is first and foremost an *American* playwright; his work straddles the United States, encompassing its farming communities, small towns, and big cities. A Southerner by birth, he has never lost sight of his early country experiences, although he now chooses to make his home in Sag Harbor, New York. He is a writer fascinated by the sheer diversity of humanity and, as he has moved from place to place and from job to job, he has amalgamated his rich experiences into a valuable and enriching dramatic style. Wherever Wilson has settled, he has used the landscape as his canvas, peopling it with dramatized composites of his friends and acquaintances, recreating and extending their language into poetic cadences, and always striving to capture truth and put it onstage.

One of Wilson's most remarkable achievements has been his ability to adapt the language of his drama to the times in which he has lived; no matter what the backdrop, Wilson's depiction is fresh and accurate. The linguistic patterns and rhythms present in works such as *The Rimers of Eldritch* and *This Is the Rill Speaking,* which are essentially written in the language of his Missouri childhood, diverge so dramatically from those used in the urban plays that they could almost be the work of another dramatist. Tanya Berezin observes that

> Lanford has moved on as a human being from one life to another and yet again to another and he is still open enough to respond artistically to all he encounters. He doesn't have to go way back [to his early days] to find his artistic life. You know that he has lived with all of these sounds and experienced and assimilated them in an extraordinary way. It is an astonishing gift.[1]

An analysis of Wilson's work reveals several recurrent themes: the necessity of retaining a sense of individual worth, the importance of personal history and the preservation of the past, and, especially, the necessity for familial support—surrogate or otherwise. These concepts run throughout the entire canon of Wilson's drama, but are nowhere more forcefully demonstrated than in the three urban plays to be considered here: *Balm in Gilead, The Hotl Baltimore* and *Burn This.*

To be true to oneself and to follow one's own instincts are all-important values in Wilson's world. As Martin J. Jacobi points out: "Wilson professes to his audiences that people can be individuals, sometimes eccentrically so, and still be good members of their group."[2] His urban plays exemplify this perfectly, but a particularly fine example can be found in *Balm in Gilead.* The drug addicts, pimps and prostitutes who inhabit the all-night café at the center of the action have formed a society with its own code of conduct. While their chosen lifestyle may be far from ideal and could even be regarded as tragic, it is, nonetheless, of their own choosing, and Wilson makes it clear that no apologies for their behavior and amoral outlook are being offered.

As far as personal history is concerned, this is linked with the necessity to preserve the past, to learn from it, and to implement change and improvements. Perhaps the best illustration of this occurs in *The Hotl Baltimore;* the action of this play is set in the lobby of an almost derelict hotel, its staff and tenants existing in a kind of half-life between the past and a very uncertain—and threatening—future. The tawdriness of their life experience is presented alongside the decrepit architecture of the Hotel, and the audience is invited to make an obvious connection between the two: what once was hopeful and, perhaps, even beautiful is now soiled and contaminated. That the characters continue to look toward a brighter future is typical of Wilson's fundamental optimism, though such optimism is occasionally soured with the taste of disappointment.

A further example can be found in *Burn This;* here, the action turns upon the sudden death of one of a group of friends and artists living in a desirable residential area of Manhattan. The past, in the guise of Robbie's death and his brother's subsequent arrival, devastates their lives but, with varying degrees of success, each character draws upon his or her personal history in an effort to deal with the present.

Wilson quotes fellow playwright Robert Patrick as observing that virtually all of Wilson's plays deal with "trying to find a perfect family."[3] Tanya Berezin concurs with this view, stating that "Lanford is very concerned with family and the way in which human beings create families when there isn't a blood family to be part of."[4] His desire to dramatize the constant need for familial grouping can even be observed in the chosen locations of these plays, although Wilson does, of course, expand the theme into their very fabric.

In *Balm in Gilead,* the comfort and familiarity offered by fellow outcasts frequenting the seedy cafe on Upper Broadway takes the place of real family ties for those who drift in and out of its never closed doors. The lobby of *The Hotl Baltimore* becomes a substitute "living room" for the young and old who rub shoulders there, make-believe parents and children whose propinquity forces interaction. The Yuppified, minimalist simplicity of the Manhattan loft in *Burn This* reflects the artistic sensibilities of its inhabitants; its sparse furnishings and almost nonexistent decoration mirror their lack of true involvement or commitment. To compensate for this emotional detachment, its tenants have formed a family of sorts, though its impermanence and fragility is made clear throughout the play.

Because of Wilson's rural roots, he brings to his urban plays a freshness of perception often missing from the work of those born and bred in the city; there is little that is hackneyed or clichéd about the scenes he presents. The brittle, rather desiccated, tone acquired by many urban playwrights is missing in Wilson's work; in his hands, life on the city streets is not so much enervating as enlivening, his portrayal of sometimes less than stalwart citizens refreshingly light and unmoralistic. Wilson once observed of his small-town based Talley plays that they were merely "a side trip that took [him] away from the line of [his] work."[5] However, something of a contradiction seems to exist here, because he has also said that these plays allowed him to "get out of New York, to write about America, and that's the America I know."[6]

This apparent dichotomy is perhaps the key to much of Wilson's work. With roots in the countryside of Missouri, he has nonetheless adopted a huge, urban metropolis as his home and clearly relishes the creative nourishment he finds there. For him, the complexity of individual characters is what is predominantly appealing; there are no generalizations to be made. The inspiration and diversity of experience he depicts in his town-dwelling characters are echoed in the far from simplistic lives of those he recalls from his childhood. He remembers the people he grew up with as being

> . . . so complicated and . . . so rich. . . . I go back and find that half the people in my high school class are divorced, and someone has murdered someone else, and so and so is cheating on such and such, and Marylou just killed her baby, and one of my best friends is now an incredible alcoholic, and the guy least likely to succeed is now practically the mayor, and . . . yet all those idyllic values I remember, the warm human values, are still there, too, existing in parallel. That's what I mean when I say it's damned complicated.[7]

Although in many ways their work could not be more different, a comparison with the dramatic undertow of some of Wilson's small-town or country-based plays could be made with the films of David Lynch, in particular *Blue Velvet* and the *Twin Peaks* saga. In Lynch's world, complexities and emotional trauma usually equal violence and terror; his is altogether a much darker view of humanity. Lynch depicts what at first seems to be a blissful and pastoral Arcadia in the white-picket-fenced, blue-skied environs of his own small towns, but no sooner is the audience lulled into a sense of false security than all preconceptions are forcefully shattered by the realisation that things are definitely not as they seem: the idyll is shown to be a nest of worms.

Nothing so bleak or vicious inhabits Wilson's rural landscapes, although a nerve-wracking sense of foreboding and terror is not unknown: in *The Rimers of Eldritch*, for example, jealousy, cowardice, lies, and murder are just a few of the vices that proliferate unseen in a quiet country town. Just as Lynch slowly reveals the rotting underbelly of his pretty havens, so too does Wilson gradually unwrap the many threads of gossip and innuendo that ravage Eldritch; in this play, nothing is clear until its closing scenes, when the truth is finally told.

Since Wilson's rural and his urban influences have made such an enormous contribution to his art, it is quite impossible for him to reject either. Now that he numbers among his friends many fellow playwrights and artists, Wilson's landscape has changed once again; he has access to yet another world—"the moneyed world."[8]

In his efforts to find suitable forms in which to express these diverse strands of drama, Wilson creates a very personal kind of theatre whose motivating force is the drive to be absolutely honest. Above all, Wilson wants to tell the truth; for him, reality is almost—but not quite—enough. By basing his dramas in his own rich life experiences, he finds little need to exaggerate. What is extraordinary about his work is his ability to recreate situations that are wholly believeable, almost documentary, while simultaneously raising them above mere realism to poetic drama. He achieves this synthesis through his complete mastery of dramatic language, whether this takes the form of creating a fully-rounded character with a few deft lines, constructing a profoundly revealing monologue, or exactly capturing a particular tone or cadence of ordinary discourse.

Eugene Ionesco once observed that one discovers more than one invents and that invention is really discovery or rediscovery. Throughout a long and prolific playwriting career, Wilson has displayed a tendency to adhere to this concept. In play after play, he has relied upon his discoveries about the human condition—and about himself. Ostensibly, verisimilitude takes precedence, even if the detail becomes fictionalized in the process, and the form the drama takes is sometimes far from realistic. All playwrights rely upon their own experiences to some extent, but for Wilson this strategy is more than an aid to creativity: it is the *raison d'être* of his drama.

Wilson has observed that his intention as a dramatist is to provide a fictionalized though basically documentary record of contemporary existence, one through which he can provide an accurate depiction of life as it is currently lived and the social mores that govern it:

> I'm trying to record my contemporary history, where we are and what I see around me today. . . . I want people to see—and to read—my plays and to say, "This is what it was like living in that place at that time. People haven't changed a damn bit. We can recognize everyone!"[9]

Elsewhere, he notes how "where we are today"[10] has always been a central concern; as an artist, he feels it is his duty to "be responsible to the times."[11] Elaborating, he states: "If I can get it down accurately, it's going to reflect something larger than the microcosm we are dealing with. . . . I write the world as I see it around me".[12]

This is not to give the impression that Wilson's work is little more than a series of sociological or anthropological tracts that include a minimum of creative input. He combines a peculiarly subtle artistry with the pragmatics of everyday life to achieve his aim, and clearly he does far more than offer verbatim representations of reality. His plays are first-rate examples of creative and resonant drama and illustrate the proficiency with which he is able to "lift ordinary speech and dance it just a little"[13] to create language that is at once as vital as real speech and as complex as dense verse.

In stating that his main concern is to provide contemporary snapshots of experience, Wilson risks undermining and underestimating his achievement as an artist. An explanation for such modesty is offered by Marshall Mason who has, perhaps, had more experience than anyone of Wilson's creative artistry:

> I think he does undersell himself. What I think he really means but doesn't say is that he is trying to keep his writing simple, to the point and incisive rather than thinking about creating "art," though he clearly does, and knows he does. If he were to start self-consciously checking what he does, he is afraid he might become self-obsessed and contrived.[14]

This is borne out by Wilson himself, who is constantly alert for any tendency to drift into obvious "artiness or pretentiousness."[15] A more obvious "artiness" is apparent in Wilson's early experimental—often rural—drama; his willingness to move beyond the established frontiers of theatre into more eclectic modes of expression was responsible for some exceptionally fecund risk-taking. In order fully to appreciate the range of his dramatic achievement, it is necessary to briefly look at the sheer range of experimentation evident in these early plays, where any surface naturalism is quickly dissipated by recurring theatrical elements such as direct audience address, the repetition of key scenes, non-chronological time frames, and unorthodox uses of stage lighting. Another favourite device is the use of clearly symbolic characters whose depiction veers more toward surrealism or impressionism. *This Is the Rill Speaking* incorporates many of these unconventional effects like stylised repetitions of dialogue, sudden shifts in locale, and scenes impinging upon and affecting one another.

Wilson could also be regarded as a literary impressionist in that he sometimes molds both dialogue and the shape of whole plays into a slowly revealed mosaic. Rather than working within a linear structure, he prefers to offer an odd glimpse of truth or an elucidation that can only be clearly appreciated from a distance, where the work can be viewed as a whole. A line of dialogue uttered early in a play that may have been evocative though confusing is later revealed as a crucial stroke in a much wider picture; a mystifying repetition at last becomes clear and vital to the whole.

Wilson appreciates the dramatic potential in deferred exposition and therefore often conceals essential truths about characters or events until late in the play. Two works that brilliantly exploit this theatrical device are *The Rimers of Eldritch* and *Stoop*. In the former, Wilson uses time as a fluid and malleable entity, combining and reordering scenes that occur in the spring, summer, and fall. The majority of the actors taking part remain onstage throughout the play, "grouping as needed to suggest time and place."[16] The action of the entire play hinges upon the death of a town scapegoat, who is despised for his voyeurism and strange sexual proclivities, but this fact is only made explicit in its closing moments. Again, some of the characters are deliberately undeveloped and serve a purely symbolic purpose in conveying Wilson's dramatic message.

In *Stoop*, it eventually becomes clear that some kind of environmental catastrophe has occurred, leaving the streets littered with dead bodies and rats, no doubt accounting for the "smell" the women complain about. Wilson thereby builds up a mosaic of events or theatrical pictures that, as the play progresses, illuminate its dramatic core.

One of Wilson's more eccentric theatrical devices is his frequent use of "unreal" characters. In *Home Free!*, for example, these are literally imaginary, unseen, and exist only in the minds of the two protagonists who play out their fantasy life to their psychologically defined friends. In *The Madness of Lady Bright*, a Boy and Girl, "both very attractive, perhaps twenty-five,"[17] share the stage, without speaking, with the increasingly hysterical Leslie. These figments of Leslie's imagination are, according to Wilson;

> used to move the action—to Leslie's memories, moods. They express, as actors, various people, voices, lovers. Sometimes they should be involved, sometimes almost bored, impatient, sometimes openly hostile, as the people he has known.[18]

After taking experimentation as far as he could in his early works, Wilson has chosen, on the whole, to reject unsettling *coups de théâtre* and other theatrical tricks and to work within a more traditional, linear structure. Thus, the majority of plays written after the mid-1960s are largely intended to be performed in a "realistic" fashion. He has stated that his move away from the experimental was a conscious and deliberate decision, since he felt he was missing valuable opportunities for character development—an area of his playwriting he was keen to improve upon:

> I had become very good at wordplay with plays like *Rimers of Eldritch;* it was too easy. I could do them without real effort and there was so little development. When *Rimers* was published, I read it and saw that Josh has seven lines; I knew so much about Josh and his is a really interesting story but it's not in the play. I wanted to move away from tricks toward real character development. I wanted to achieve something deeper . . . to see how deep it's possible to go into people . . . to still get the sociology and the politics but also to get depth of character.[19]

Just how successful Wilson has been in achieving this aim can be seen in every play in which character has been the primary and defining factor. In mainly choosing to write about those who have been described as "outsiders," but who are described by him as survivors, Wilson's writing has become finely focused. These are people who carry on despite disadvantage or poverty and are, in his opinion, deserving of our admiration. For Wilson, they are far more interesting than the rank and file who toe the line and preserve societal norms. The undefined sense of exclusion generally experienced by such characters is exemplified by Millie in *The Hotl Baltimore,* who observes that "I've always thought of myself as a bit outside of society: I never seem to understand what other people expect" (act 1, p. 21).

Surveying recurrent elements in Wilson's drama, Mel Gussow describes the playwright's most frequent creations as

> the wounded and the wistful, those who cling to their illusions as if they are identity cards, who never stop searching for solutions. . . . Undiscouraged by disappointment, they continue to nurture private dreams. . . . They project such a purity of spirit—idealism honed to perfection—that, in comparison, conformists seem like aliens.[20]

Wilson feels an affinity with and understands such people, having lived among them for a considerable period. Constant throughout his drama is a compassionate interest in humanity in all its diversity, and an appreciation of this fact is essential to an understanding of his work. Wilson portrays people *as they are;* refusing to glamourize or falsify them in any way, he depicts them as individuals.

Wilson's gallery of social deviants and eccentrics is extensive and varied, but similar characters do reappear throughout his work: the cunning hustlers, stoic, golden-hearted whores, disenchanted lovers, and feisty homosexuals reappear again and again. Emotionally wounded though seldom beaten down by life, they may be fragile, but usually retain a tough and durable core, and are quite capable of surviving in a raw and hostile world. It is difficult not to feel compassion for these individuals, even at their most self-indulgent or irritating; they are so recognisably human that audience identification is almost guaranteed.

However, not all of Wilson's characters are candidates for outright affection; in particular, the gossipping and venal *Rimers of Eldritch* are far from appealing. Perhaps the denizens of this work, with their small-town mentalities and cruel dispositions, represent the least sympathetic of any of Wilson's creations. Here, he portrays a vicious world in which innocent people are hounded and betrayed, and where the vicious perpetrators seem to thrive despite their sins. A deep pessimism over humanity's ability to redeem itself is evident, but this is uncharacteristic of Wilson's work, especially as far as the characters themselves are concerned.

Wilson usually rejects cynicism in favour of compassion, remaining nonjudgmental and impartial, looking for the good in everyone. He tends to give even the most undeserving the benefit of the doubt, and he maintains, throughout his work, a sense of loyalty toward those he dramatizes. Much of Wilson's best writing is reserved for his least (ostensibly) attractive creations; like Sam Shepard and David Mamet, he finds poetry in their often denuded and inarticulate utterances. He seems to share the playwriting strategy of Friedrich Hebbel, who averred that "in the drama, what we shall see as bad we must also be able to see as good. The problematic is the life breath of poetry."[21]

The cautious optimism found in the majority of Wilson's plays is certainly absent from *Serenading Louie*, a deeply pessimistic and disturbing work written in the early 1970s. Those portrayed here hail from a more affluent social stratum than many of his characters, and they are all fairly successful in their careers, if not in their personal lives. When Carl murders his wife and then commits suicide, the audience is invited to blame not only him, but also his victim and the society that has driven them toward a tragic end. Here Wilson implies that *everyone* is a misfit, whatever their social class, since the world we inhabit offers no chance of peace or sense of community.

The play had a devastating effect upon those who saw it, inducing tears and feelings of deep depression; Wilson recalls how, at the end of some performances of the piece,

> the audience lined up with tranquilizers in the palms of their hands at the water fountain; they were shaking, trembling. And [in another production] children would be running crying up and down the aisles because they recognized their parents onstage. . . . I realized then that this wasn't why I was a playwright—I didn't want to ruin their evening![22]

After this experience, he decided that his plays would in future be of a more sanguine nature and that he would "find something more positive to say."[23] Additionally, he has recently observed that he "always distrusted the pessimism in the work."[24]

However, despite the fact that Wilson subsequently rejected this desperate view of the world, the fact that it was so powerfully depicted is instructive. If, at that time, he viewed all of humanity as dysfunctional or nonintegrative due to the lack of a sympathetic and caring society, it points to another reason why he so frequently depicts outsiders in their most obvious forms. Wilson's "survivors" are extreme symbols of us all. During an interview, he confirmed that a crucial element in his dramatization of such individuals is that, by concentrating upon the extremes of experience, he can point to the universal rather than to the particular.

With *Lemon Sky*, his most autobiographical work to date, Wilson ceased (with one or two exceptions) to write plays that dealt with the kind of misfits who had hitherto so frequently peopled his work. Here, he wrote directly about himself as an outsider in his own family and seemingly underwent a kind of catharsis. According to Marshall Mason, "by directly confronting the issues raised in the work, he somehow obviated the need to continue to write about outsiders."[25]

While it is true that Wilson no longer writes about the disenfranchised group that typified his early work, the concept of the outsider persists, but in a different form; the protagonists may be wealthy establishment figures or brilliant artists but, in some crucial—if covert—respect, they remain apart from the rest of society. In the world Wilson creates, even his geniuses are outsiders, as exemplified by Dr. Don in *Angels Fall*, Gerri Riordan in *Redwood Curtain*, or Robbie in *Burn This*. Mason notes:

> In a funny kind of way, Lanford's new play, *Redwood Curtain*, again deals with outsiders, but only in one respect in the accepted sense of the word. Here we have a combination of extremes because, on the one hand we have a tremendously well-established and connected family, and on the other we follow the story of their adopted half-Vietnamese daughter who is a piano prodigy but feels unfulfilled; she is trying to discover who she is because she feels excluded in some inner kind of way. In the same play is the classic outsider—the man who may be her real father—who is a Vietnam veteran who wanders around the redwood forest, unable to assimilate back into society.[26]

In many of his plays, Wilson portrays outsiders such as sexual nonconformists; homosexuals and lesbians recur in works as diverse as *The Madness of Lady Bright*, the *Fifth of July*, *The Hotl Balitmore*, *Balm in Gilead* and *Burn This*. Wilson obviously enjoys writing about these individuals, and his pleasure is reflected in the wonderfully sharp, wry, and insightful dialogue with which he usually provides them. That they are often misunderstood or maligned by conventional society is fully comprehended by Wilson, and he ensures that they do not suffer similar discrimination within the scope of his drama. He peoples his plays with individuals of diverse sexual persuasions not because he wishes to shock, but merely because they are part of life. As Tanya Berezin observes:

> He uses such people in his plays because they are part of everything. . . . it is the larger world. . . . There are some wonderful playwrights who don't include people like that because they just don't have a world view, but Lanford does. It's part of what *is*.[27]

Similarly, Lou Liberatore (Larry in the London productions of *Burn This*) notes:

> The world is not a gay world. It's not a straight world. It's both. It's life. There's room for everything. . . . These are the people Lanford chooses to write about; whether they are gay or straight is irrelevant.[28]

There are of course many plays that incorporate or are based upon homosexual characters, but this does not mean that homosexuality is their only subject. Harvey Fierstein's *Torch Song Trilogy* may be centered around the life and times of a drag performer, but its dramatic reach is surely much broader: it touches on such themes as parental disapproval and betrayal, loneliness, the need both to give and to receive affection, duplicity among friends, and the belief that an individual's sexuality should not preclude them from parenthood. Similar complexities could be read into plays as diverse as Christopher Marlowe's *Edward II*, Martin Sherman's *Bent*, or Tony Kushner's *Angels in America*. Of *The Madness of Lady Bright*, Wilfrid Sheed notes that

> . . . as with *Death in Venice*, it ceases to be of fundamental importance that the focus is homosexual. The subject is human loneliness, abandonment, cyclic betrayal.[29]

Another variety of Wilson's nonconformists occurs most compellingly in *Burn This* in the character of Pale. Well-dressed and affluent, Pale is a married man with two children and a responsible job as a restaurant manager. Appearances can, however, be deceptive. Pale is also a habitual drug-user and probable alcoholic who can barely control the contempt and anger he feels for the world;

he is mercurial, volatile, and given to eruptions of sporadic violence. An explosive rebel, Pale is desperate to escape the confines
of his life.

Wilson also sometimes portrays outsiders who lead almost unbearably tragic lives, caught up in an emotional maelstrom entirely of their own making. Perhaps the ultimate example of this
occurs in *Home Free!*. In this work, the incestuous brother and
sister have, with the exception of essential shopping trips, severed
all connections with the outside world. Behind closed doors, they
nurture and develop their romantic fantasies, playing childish
games and inventing imaginary companions. Joanna is pregnant
with her brother's child, but the pair seem unable to comprehend
the seriousness of their situation. Tragedy suddenly invades their
closeted fantasy world when Joanna is taken ill, and the agorapho-
bic Lawrence cannot bring himself to fetch medical help. As a
result of his inaction, she dies for want of treatment.

It is clear that people fascinate Wilson; their sheer diversity
yet essential similarity obsess him. The loneliness, sadness, and
poignant aspiration he has observed in the most down-at-heel of
his characters are clearly echoed by their more socially advan-
taged opposites. Thus, the need for affection and understanding
craved by many of his damaged prostitutes recurs in an ostensibly
sophisticated and affluent woman (Anna in *Burn This*), and the
sense of isolation and helplessness visible in a slow-witted
emotionally retarded, and poverty-stricken youngster (Jamie in
The Hotl Baltimore) is reprised with much sardonic and self-
deprecatory wit in a well-heeled, homosexual advertising execu-
tive (Larry in *Burn This*).

The montage-like, surreal, and disjointed structure of Wilson's
early plays—typified by *Balm in Gilead*—is reflected in their subject
matter and characterization. He mainly depicted lost and deracinated individuals whose complete assimilation into an amoral and
very harsh counterculture reflected his somewhat pessimistic view
of the world. Society had no place for these characters, and their
reaction to it was often one of hostility and distrust.

Over the years, however, Wilson's views have become more optimistic, and he has tended to concentrate upon individuals who,
while continuing to challenge societal norms, nevertheless find a
place in society. Examples of such characters include Ken, the
crippled homosexual Vietnam veteran in *Fifth of July;* the embit-

tered, atheistic Dealer in *Brontosaurus;* and the Mexican Indian Dr. Don in *Angels Fall,* who is forced to choose between maintaining his ethnic roots and thereby continuing his rather primitive medical practice in a remote outpost and the opportunity to leave for the big city, where he will research a possible cure for cancer.

Wilson invites and expects our empathy and, usually, our acceptance of his characters without criticism. His uncritical stance no doubt stems from his affection for them, but some critics believe that this tendency destroys, or at least dilutes, dramatic tension and often leads to sentimentality and bathos. For example, Edith Oliver opines of the tragicomic *The Madness of Lady Bright* that it is full of "shameless, old-fashioned mawkishness"[30] in its depiction of an aging and hysterical drag performer whose sexual charms diminish daily. Her opinion concerning the quality of Wilson's work remained unchanged by *The Hotl Baltimore;* she observed that "it has a synthetic ring and is very sentimental."[31] Gerald Weales is similarly disparaging, describing Wilson as "the schmaltziest of the up-from-off-off-Broadway playwrights"[32] and denigrating his "tonal softness".[33]

Because Wilson's drama often explores the extremes of emotion and the situations in which his characters interact occasionally lean toward the melodramatic, some excess or overstatement is almost inevitable. However, this does not automatically mean a lapse into bathetic exaggeration—merely an emphasis on emotion or sadness. Far from relying upon easy options or maudlin emotionalism, Wilson is at pains to avoid creeping sentimentality, even though it *is* difficult to adopt a detached standpoint when writing about those to whom one has a close emotional attachment.

He has stated that he personally loathes mawkishness in any form and is at great pains to eliminate it from his writing, even in extreme moments. About a potentially sentimental situation in *The Hotl Baltimore,* when Jackie verbally protects her brother, Wilson states that he deliberately avoided any descent into overt emotionalism:

When Jackie stands up for Jamie, I made sure that her speech was pared right down, with no easy sentiment. It still gets the point across. Of course it could have been awful, mawkish, but it isn't. I wish critics could be with me when I'm writing—for them to see how far I *could* go would be instructive.[34]

Marshall Mason also rejects any suggestion of sentimentality in Wilson's work, observing that this implies that

the emotions revealed and examined in his plays are not earned. They are *always* earned, often at great personal cost. One of Lanford's greatest achievements is the uncompromising determination he demonstrates in order to dramatize this process; it is not sentimental, but an attempt to find the truth.[35]

It would seem that critics who decry Wilson's drama because of its apparent sentimentality miss both the irony and humor in his work. It is true that he frequently dramatizes sad, even tragic, situations, but these are almost never without a leavening injection of humor, no matter how bleak. Certainly Anna's experience at Robbie's funeral in *Burn This* is traumatic in the extreme, but this does not prevent Wilson from extricating every possible nuance of comedy from the débâcle—from the family's mistaken identity of Anna as the gay Robbie's "girlfriend" to the ludicrous, though sinister, episode in her bedroom when the butterflies pinned to the walls revive and begin to beat their wings. The fact that Sally in *Fifth of July* carries around the ashes of her dead husband in a box provides another opportunity to indulge in a little gallows humor, as do the pathetic, though hilarious, vocal wanderings of the drugged Dopey and Fick in *Balm in Gilead*. Realizing that outright pathos is sometimes insufficient to convey a dramatic point, Wilson continues to insert humor into the blackest of moments and, in the process, frees them from sentimental excess and transforms them into touching comedy.

Another criticism of Wilson's work is a perceived lack of resolve in his characters; it is claimed that they *choose* not to improve their lives, but to wallow in self-pity and bathos, helpless victims whose destiny is out of their control, with little impetus to amelioration. While it is true that their future may be unaffected by any action they may take, these characters are seldom near despair. In spite of all that life throws at them, they retain a sense of optimism and continue to dream of the future.

A cursory viewing may suggest indifference or resignation, but careful analysis reveals something quite different. Thus, most of the residents of, say, the *The Hotl Baltimore* may appear content to pass their days lethargically as the hotel crumbles around them, but they do continue to harbor vague notions that the future will bring more luck and a better way of life—even if the past is more reliable for solace and comfort. Similarly, those who people the sleazy café in *Balm in Gilead* might compromise any chance of true happiness or deliverance by their reliance upon an easy drug deal or the "entertainment" of yet another client, but they do maintain a belief that their current lot is only temporary and that better times must be ahead.

Furthermore, the bleakness of these characters' lives is an established "given" of the play itself, like the destinies meted out to the protagonists of Tom Stoppard's *Rosencrantz and Guildenstern Are Dead* or of Eugene O'Neill's *The Iceman Cometh*. Wilson's characters stay where they are, indulging in vague pipe dreams of future happiness, because the essence of the drama is their impotence and inability to change within a hostile society. There is also the suggestion that even those who *do* move on probably go from bad to worse, no doubt perpetuating their delusions elsewhere.

A completely antithetical criticism is offered by Henry Schvey who, ironically, believes Wilson's characters share an "unreasonable faith"[36] in the future, unfavorably comparing them with similar individuals in Chekhov. He observes that Chekhov's characters also look forward to better days but that *their* hopes are offset by the audience's perception that "the characters exist in a world where hope is not always enough,"[37] whereas Wilson's drama contains no such irony.

Schvey's perception of Wilson's dramatic intention would appear to diverge considerably from the writer's. Wilson, too, realises that "hope is not always enough": that is exactly the point of many of his plays, and their audience must surely be aware that what he is dramatizing is far from unblinkered optimism. While Wilson may retain faith in the possibility of eventual change, his work is nonetheless replete with an ironic sense of life's harsh realities. He makes it very plain that many of his characters are naive, often desperate, dreamers, who continue to believe that happier times are ahead. Whether or not their hopes will actually bear fruit is deliberately left unclear. What is important, however, is the fact that they *continue* to believe in an uncertain future, no matter how far down the social scale they have fallen. This is not gross sentimentality, but an honest depiction of an admirable human trait.

Wilson's creative and original use of language is, perhaps, his most notable achievement as a dramatist. He is, rightly, lauded for the accuracy with which he captures the rhythms and cadences of ordinary discourse, and his ability to turn even the most demotic and raw speech into a kind of vibrant poetry runs in his work from the earliest plays to the latest. Over the years, his manipulation of language has moved from a somewhat self-conscious reliance on poetic techniques to mastery of the most sophisticated badinage. Marshall Mason notes:

> From the very beginning, Lanford demonstrated a remarkable musical gift in terms of poetry of language; he could always take ordinary everyday speech and lift it out of the prosaic. In his early work, there was great emphasis on fairly *obvious* poetry and experimentation with language but, as he developed as a writer, this became much more refined. The poetry still exists but it is now seamless and totally integrates into the flow of the dialogue.[38]

For Tanya Berezin, Wilson's abilities with language can be summed up thus: "Going out with Lanford, having lunch or dinner with him, standing on the street, you can *see* him hearing the music of people's language and registering in his computer ear. He is constantly aware of the sounds going on around him."[39]

Describing her perception, as an actress, of his mastery of language, Berezin elaborates:

> Performing his work is extraordinary, because making those sounds in your mouth is almost like eating a chocolate éclair—it's so rich. If you relax and stay open to the language, it is impossible not to experience what the character is experiencing. A good example is T. K. Erikson in *The Mound Builders,* whom I played. This woman is an extremely articulate, brilliant writer, and her brilliance and bite is contained in every word of dialogue. Speaking the words, it was possible to believe one possessed the same qualities![40]

Even those who find his work sentimental or melodramatic recognize the quality of his linguistic abilities; Edith Oliver, a long-time detractor of Wilson's work observes that "there is no doubt . . . that he is a writer, in a profession crowded with non-writers."[41]

Those who regard Wilson's achievement more positively proclaim his gifts vociferously. Harold Clurman notes: "Wilson's writing is salty and vivid; his observation accurate and compassionate, marked by a not entirely poisonous humor. The verisimilitude does not descend to crass naturalism."[42]

As ever, Wilson seeks to record the truth, and to depict the language people use in as accurate a manner as possible, including any idiosyncrasies, slang, and non sequiturs, as well as rhythm and verbal shading. However, as an artist he strives to do far more than merely record, though there are occasions when he does just that, as in Fick's monologue in *Balm in Gilead*. Emile Zola once stressed the need for realistic-*sounding* dialogue onstage, if truth in the theatre is to be achieved, observing:

> What I want to hear in the theatre is spoken language. If we [could] reproduce on the stage a conversation with its repetitions, its length, and its useful words, the emotion and tone of the conversation could be kept; the individual turn of mind of each speaker, the reality, in a word, reproduced to the necessary extent.[43]

Wilson certainly adheres to this aim, always trying to combine real speech with a sense of lyricism. He is renowned for what has been described as poetic realism; taking ordinary discourse as his tool, he molds what are often distorted and corrupted shards of speech into strangely evocative, though often far from mellifluous, verse:

> I try to write speeches that sound the way people sound. If you were to listen to a transcript of a conversation that had been taped, it would be quite different, of course, but my work is closer to that kind of approach than that of many writers. But I am very attracted to the natural poetry in speech, and especially different characters from different backgrounds/regions of the country. I've always wanted to reproduce that in some poetic sense. The rhythm of the whole thing and the play as a whole should have the same kind of rhythm that results from the juxtaposition of all the other rhythms. So I think of it very much as writing music and telling the story at the same time. It's kind of like rubbing your tummy and patting your head at the same time.[44]

Marshall Mason describes the playwright's utilization of "poetic realism" as follows:

> It is not something Lanford invented, but it is something he happens to do awfully well. . . . it is a kind of realism that I feel is the voice of the native American theatre but it is realism that is elevated in its language. It takes the language people speak and makes it more musical.[45]

Wilson's penchant for revealing the dramatic potential in even the most banal speech can be demonstrated in a simple line from *Serenading Louie* when Mary describes her feelings for her husband, Carl: "I don't actually think that I loved him then, but I loved him then—now." (act 2, p. 41). Citing this as a particularly fine example of Wilson's linguistic creativity, John Simon observes that "I can't think of any other living American playwright who could have written a line this subtle and penetrating, this pregnant and this painful, in such utterly simple, denuded language. It is heartbreaking."[46]

Elsewhere, he also praises Wilson's ability to write "intelligent, amusing, racy dialogue."[47]

A brief selection from Wilson's drama may give some indication of his ability to find the poetry in everyday speech. In *The Madness of Lady Bright,* we witness the aging drag queen, Leslie, sorrowfully—though with much sardonic humor—raving in his room over his desperate loneliness and the short-lived lovers who have momentarily impinged upon his sadness. As he scans the walls covered with hundreds of names, he addresses some of them, as though the person to whom they belonged were actually present:

> *Leslie.* . . . Michael, it's no fun. It's no fun living here in this stupid apartment by myself listening to my few records and the neighbor's radio; I should like someone, I think sometimes, [Being delicate] living here some times. Or maybe somehow not living here but coming here to see me often. Then I'd wash the walls—wash off everyone else. Wash them off and kiss them good-by—good riddance. (p 85)

There is great poignancy here; the very fact that Leslie is reduced to speaking aloud to the written scrawls adorning his room is sad enough, but Wilson imbues his words with more than bathetic excess. The fact that he can hear his neighbor's radio indicates the shabbiness of Leslie's apartment; little privacy exists.

Even though he is alone, he maintains a sense of decorum, being "delicate" in his veiled suggestion of sexual intimacy, his desire that someone should live with him, or merely visit, "some times". Wilson's division of the word lends it extra weight and makes us reflect on the cautious dreams of Leslie, who dare not ask for too much, even within the realm of a fantasy—only that on *some* occasions he should have the company he so craves. Should such a dream come true, Leslie will "wash the walls" and, in so doing, rid himself of painful memories. Without the hundreds of signatures to remind him constantly of past indiscretions and outright folly, perhaps he could start again.

In *Days Ahead,* an unnamed man speaks to his dead wife (who, it would seem, is located behind a bricked-up wall) of the shades of memory and of their life together. Visiting her on a regular basis, he works through a calendar, describing events for her "interest":

> The note for May is a gathering. Mrs. Fields. A small party, rather the same crowd. You'll remember three years ago I mentioned the Fields had done their living room over in rust. Rust everywhere. Sepia, she called it. Looked like rust; rust everywhere. Well, they have lately changed from rust to milky-green. Milky-green everywhere. Can you picture it? It makes one quite long for the rust back again. And that was May. (p. 67)

While the poetry here may be rather self-conscious, with its obvious references to desuetude and decomposition in the color schemes mentioned, the piece retains a haunting power, due not least to the context in which the words are spoken. The repetitions "rust everywhere" and "Milky-green everywhere" create a hypnotic rhythm not diminished by the prosaic nature of the description. Wilson's economy of expression, his careful choice of imagery and color to express mood and emotional state, together with the almost casual conversational tone, combine to raise this short extract into something approaching verse.

The *Fifth of July* is full of evocative poetic imagery. A good example occurs in the war-damaged Ken's recollection of how he and his friends spent their youth, when disability and pain were the furthest things from their minds:

> *Ken.* . . . when we were very young, we were very merry, we rode back
> and forth all night on the Sausalito ferry, snorting snow. Snow was
> cocaine, and very dear, even then. (act 1, p. 13)

The liberal use of commas in the long, fluid opening sentence
concludes with precise rhythm in a short pointed coda. The combination of the two adds a musical flow to Ken's happy memory,
the first words of which echo a famous poem by Edna St. Vincent
Millay. The repetition and parallelism in the words "when we were
very young, we were very merry" point to Ken's association of the
two concepts in his mind. One could not exist without the other:
youth meant happiness, fun without responsibility, and freedom
from care. That his and his companions' idea of such fun was
associated with drugs neatly places the memory in a specific
time—the 1960s, when unbridled experimentation and absolute
liberty were the order of the day. In so few words, Wilson manages
to sum up an era, the end of an era, and interminable sadness,
all ending in Ken's wistful recollection that "Snow . . . was very
dear, even then."

The language Wilson uses is suffused with sensory appeal; as
a poet, he ensures that the lyrical and associative value of every
word he writes is utilized to the full. The intensity of his characterization and his evocation of every nuance of mood could never be
achieved by a reliance upon prosaic reality.

Looking back over his literary influences and what has inspired
him, Wilson recalls:

> One of the things that influenced me most of all was that many years
> ago I read somewhere that Arthur Miller took the essence of a charac-
> ter's speech and turned it into poetry. I thought, wow, what a wonder-
> ful thing to do and so I got a Miller play and read it and thought,
> "no, he doesn't." However, it sure would be a nice thing to do, and I
> think I have always been trying to do that, to make poetry out of
> the dialogue.[48]

His use of overlapping dialogue provides a further example of
the combination of a surface realism with lyrical creativity. Keen
to convey a sense of realism onstage, Wilson frequently uses overlapping speech like music, to create rhythms between speakers
that, once set up, form a curiously dreamlike atmosphere. Out of

a linguistic soup full of confusion and repetition, a new kind of theatrical verisimilitude is created. Wilson observes:

> I was impatient with you-talk-then-I'll-talk-then-you'll-talk-then-I'll-talk. So many people around me talk at the same time, they are all yelling and screaming, saying "No, no, no, me, me, me." I was attracted to the idea of putting that onstage.[49]

In his films *M*A*S*H* and *Nashville,* and, more recently, *The Player,* Robert Altman did something similar, with characters constantly interrupting each other and speaking over other conversations. This created a melee of sound that many film critics and audiences found disorientating, but others found hypnotic and fascinating. It certainly added verisimilitude to these films, which were set in a mobile army hospital unit, at a country music festival and in high-powered Hollywood offices, respectively. The technique proves particularly effective in Wilson's *Balm in Gilead,* the vaguely surreal atmosphere in the all-night café providing another perfect location for such experimentation.

Wilson's carefully developed verbal structures and linguistic arias have led to much comment upon his drama's musicality. He explains that this probably stems from his experiences as a singer in the chorus at high school: he was—and is—very fond of choral music. John O'Connor observes:

> The most outstanding ingredient in all of the Wilson plays is an extraordinary use of language, the ability to compose not so much patches of interesting dialogue as sustained series of quiet lyricism, resembling vocal duets, trios, or complex ensemble pieces.[50]

Speaking of *This Is the Rill Speaking,* Martin Gottfried refers to Wilson's sometimes experimental use of language:

> . . . it was an early example of a movement away from the intelligibility of dialogue. This sounds silly, but if you listen carefully there is an overlap to daily conversation that turns meaningful words into the beat and music of existence itself. Wilson grasped the feel and rhythm of human conversation.[51]

Lou Liberatore compares Wilson's writing not only with music but with dance: "Lanford's dialogue is like choreography. It is very heightened writing. . . . although it is realistic in a kind of poetic way, it is also very heightened, operatic and almost like a ballet."[52]

Similarly, Marshall Mason recalls that, in his direction of *The Hotl Baltimore,* he "almost choreographed the movement of the people, because there really is music to it. If the people don't move in a musical way, then it's impossible to keep focused."[53]

Wilson's manipulation of language is especially impressive in what Friedrich Hebbel calls the "pure respirations of the soul"[54]— monologues. Wilson is very fond of this kind of exposition, explaining it as a "literary interest,"[55] and has observed that he has always seen writing monologues as a good test of his creative abilities:

> I have always been drawn to them; they're a real challenge. Monologues are a good way of honing one's writing; what is important is to make them as arty as you possibly can without ever *sounding* arty, because the second one word sounds contrived, I'm up and out of there. The goal is to write something well, that doesn't sound wrong and is real and right for the moment and means something pertinent.[56]

Monologues are used to a large extent in his early works, and superb examples can be found in *Balm in Gilead.* Here, Wilson demonstrates his versatility in capturing exactly the correct tone and cadence, whether the speaker is a semi-articulate drug addict whose brain-addled verbosity is shot through with exactly the right amount of imprecise fantasy and denuded articulation or a dim-witted prostitute whose sentimentalized memories of what was surely a tawdry and sorry "love" affair speak volumes about her naiveté and credulousness.

Wilson has often been designated an "actor's playwright." All dramatists, by virtue of their craft, write with actors in mind, but this is particularly true of Wilson. His predilection for creating parts for actors has persisted since the founding of the Circle Repertory Company. He explains how, when writing *The Hotl Baltimore:*

> I looked around [Circle Repertory] and tried to use as many of the Circle actors as possible. As soon as I got a character in mind, I was able to say who should play it. Every character in that play was written for a particular actor.[57]

Wilson believes that this process keeps his work firmly rooted in reality and prevents him from becoming pretentious; it also focuses his writing on characterization rather than theatrical experiment. Writing for specific actors is certainly not without precedent: back in the 1930s, during his work with the Group Theatre, Clifford Odets studied his fellow actors, so that he could create characters who were based in reality. Similarly, Chekhov often wrote parts for his wife, and both Shakespeare and Molière used members of their immediate entourage for inspiration.

Wilson's understanding of and affection for actors is consistent with the playwriting strategy he has adopted since his early days with the Circle Repertory Company. Because he is willing to experiment, Wilson's performers are given enormous freedom and are constantly encouraged to discover the truth of their roles. Wilson attends as many rehearsals as possible. Keen to ensure that his texts sound real, unforced, and unmannered, he will frequently have actors read his scripts aloud without acting the parts. Lou Liberatore recalls how, during the rehearsals for the American production of *Burn This,* Wilson spent hours with the actors, going over their lines, changing and editing:

> He was there every day! . . . If we had a problem with a line or whatever, if there was a rhythm or a phrase that caught the ear in a certain way and it didn't quite work, he would always change it. He would change anything that didn't sound *just right.*[58]

Similarly, Christopher Reeve observes that Wilson is never impatient: "There is never a sense that he is cooling his heels waiting for you to get it right. . . . he seems eager to watch actors discover things in his plays."[59]

Wilson thus consistently demonstrates a great affection for actors and, as Don Shewey has noted, "will describe performances over fifteen years ago as if he saw them yesterday and supply a running commentary on their palpable effect."[60]

The tag, "actors playwright," also refers to Wilson's ability to write dialogue that actors enjoy speaking. He has an almost uncanny ability to create dialogue that is eminently *speakable,* without any sense of falsity or pretension. He is, according to one critic, simply "damned good at dialogue. The talk is not only listenable but, to the players' obvious pleasure, sayable."[61]

Michael Simkins, who played Burton in the London production of *Burn This,* comments on the endlessly adaptable text that Wilson provides, which affords actors numerous interpretative strategies:

> Wilson's writing is vivid and alive, particularly in the way it relates to actors. It allows you to interpret, to create. The last scene in *Burn This* between Burton and Larry is such a fabulously written scene. . . . Lou [Liberatore] and I found that we could nudge the scene different ways on different nights according to whether one of us was feeling slightly angry, slightly melancholy, or slightly happy. And the scene would react. It would go with you. . . . it was like it was on an invisible cushion and you could just push it and it would go and it would still work.[62]

The craft of creating dialogue is equated by Wilson with that of acting:

> . . . it is . . . observation of the outside, filtered through things you have experienced yourself. You know intuitively what it's like having something stolen or stealing something or being a member of a minority race, because there are specific instances in your life where you were that person in a certain situation. Actors remember that moment, while they are playing a particular scene, and that's how they get this incredible truth. It's the same thing for me.[63]

Wilson will occasionally deliberately write a difficult or unlikely part for his players as a challenge to any preconceived notions they may hold about themselves. Such roles are intended to coerce them into exploring facets of their personality usually kept hidden. Tanya Berezin, for example, felt that she was quite incapable of playing intelligent or humorous characters, thereby significantly reducing the number of roles she could take on in Wilson's work. To eradicate her doubts, Wilson created a role for her which combined these elements—"a part . . . about an intelligent woman who is very funny."[64] The role became central to *The Mound Builders,* and Ms. Berezin won an Obie for her efforts.

Similarly, the part of the Priest in *Angels Fall* was written specifically for Barnard Hughes, an actor unused to such spiritual roles. However, it gave him the opportunity to explore the full range of his talent, and the result was, according to Tanya Berezin, "quite wonderful".[65] Wilson thus enjoys looking beyond the usual process of casting actors to "type," preferring instead to develop challenging—often unnerving—contrasts. More frequently, however, he appears to draw heavily upon actors' individual and idiosyncratic talents and will often shape a role that either condenses or expands certain key elements of a particular performer's personality.

What he has discovered in actors as individuals *informs* his work, but that is not to say that the *parts* he creates for them are themselves little more than literary versions of the actors' personalities. Wilson has the ability to write a part for an actor, while never attempting to "capture" their essence—which he sees as a fruitless and impossible quest. He has observed that someone may give him an idea for a particular character but that, once the idea has become established in his mind, pure invention takes over:

> When you get deeply into a character you are inventing a lot; once I get the rhythm of the character and the parameters of his or her concern, I can riff on that for days. I can invent things that that person would never have thought of. You can't ever "get" the person because that's impossible, but I can get my own version of it.[66]

Michael Warren Powell confirms the impossibility of "capturing" the essence of an individual:

> It is just not possible—it's such an abstract concept. Actors can't always act roles that are written for them. Whatever that mysterious thing is that the writer sensed in them, the actor often has no idea how to tap into that, into someone's concept of who they are and how they speak. When it happens, as with John Malkovich in *Burn This,* it's brilliant, but it doesn't always work. . . . A role was once written for me and I was brought back from Spain especially to do it. I read it and said, "I don't get it," and the writer said, "Well, it's you." But what does that *mean?* I could never do that role.[67]

Thus, Wilson never attempts exactly to match facets of actors' personalities when he writes for them, but he may write with a particular individual in mind, seeing something in the actor that he would like to develop.

Another side of this process occurs when characters begin to assume a life of their own and direct the playwright. An excellent example occurs in *Angels Fall:*

> The characters tell *you.* If you're writing well, you can't make them do things you want them to do half the time. All through this play, I knew that Don [the Indian doctor] was going to stay; at the end, he gets up and walks out! You can tell them exactly what to do, *exactly* how to live their lives and they say "that's incredibly inspiring," and get up and do what they were going to do anyway. I didn't know that Don would leave until the very last page. Of course he does; it's obvious.[68]

Wilson's drama has been frequently compared to that of Tennessee Williams; but Wilson believes his own work to be far removed in quality from that of one of his main literary heroes and formative influences:

> He [Williams] is great, and I'm not. . . . If I'm that good, I don't want to know about it. I have to live. It's why I focus on writing for specific actors, working on specific things, and not on the hoopla. You can't live up to hoopla.[69]

He can see very few similarities between his own and Williams's work and believes that they are grouped together merely because of their geographic origins. Moreover, he has observed that "Williams writes only about sex whereas I write only about work!"[70] Although this is a gross simplification, it contains much truth; both the metaphor of work—and work itself—has certainly been an important thread through nearly all of Wilson's drama. For example, *The Mound Builders* is almost exclusively concerned with work, deriving from the emphasis on archaeology and its impact on the Indians; *Burn This* concentrates to a large extent on Anna's work as a dancer and choreographer; the antiques emporium presided over by the Dealer in *Brontosaurus* clearly has a poetic resonance, like the fashion business built up by Louise in *The Great Nebula in Orion;* the careers of the protagonists in *Serenading Louie* play a significant part in the development of the play and, in some respects, the rather spurious work carried out by the inhabitants of the café in *Balm in Gilead* shapes and controls their lives.

According to Wilson, another major difference between his and Williams's work is that, while his prime concern is to capture the dramatic and poetic essence of a particular social milieu and to portray this as truthfully and objectively as possible, almost as a documentary record of events, "Tennessee writes about his life. All of his plays are metaphors for where he is now."[71] Although at first sight there appears to be something of a contradiction here, since Wilson, too, writes about "where he is now", there are clear differences between the work of the two men. Whereas Wilson tends to stand outside the scenes he creates, casting a fairly objective eye over the proceedings, Williams is far more subjective and is usually metaphorically present in his work. He writes far more about *himself* than does Wilson, using characters such as Brick in *Cat on a Hot Tin Roof* or Blanche DuBois in *A Streetcar Named Desire* as symbols for his own experiences. Indeed, Wilson observes that he believes Williams's work can be "egotistical."[72]

It could, however, be argued that Wilson puts a similarly disguised form of himself in some of his works. This is certainly true of *Lemon Sky*, and in the character of the Girl in *The Hotl Baltimore*, and it is possible that the naive country girl Darlene in *Balm in Gilead* could be a rather obvious metaphor for himself during his early days in New York. On the whole, however, Wilson seems to resist the temptation of writing disguised variations of himself in his work.

Although a superficial connection exists between Wilson's and Williams's drama, Wilson cites Charles Dickens, rather than the American dramatist, as one of his strongest influences. The underlying complexity and extreme ambition of many of Dickens's plots, his myriad of interacting and conflicting characters, his strong moral standpoints, and his frequent excursions into the furthest reaches of melodrama have all clearly influenced Wilson. Like Dickens, he demonstrates concern for social issues and is something of a polemicist; metaphorically heightened messages about the unhappy state of the world abound in the works of both men. By comparison, melodrama in the work of Tennessee Williams pales into insignificance alongside the Victorian novelist. Wilson states, with some glee, that "Dickens is absolutely outrageous. . . . his characters are so extreme, far more than any that I have ever written—or could ever write".[73]

Extremes are seldom found in the work of two dramatists with whom Wilson is also sometimes compared: Thornton Wilder and William Inge. Again, Wilson disagrees with this perception, seeing little comparison between their drama and his own, although he has adapted certain traits found in their work to his own advantage, for example, the direct audience address and unconventional staging characteristic of a number of Wilder's plays, especially *Our Town,* and the "snowbound" play that brings together in a confined space a group of disparate characters, as exemplified by Inge's *Bus Stop.*

As for addressing the audience, Wilson identifies a production of Joan Littlewood's *The Hostage* he saw in Chicago as probably the most important influence on his use of it. Another influence was undoubtedly Williams's *The Glass Menagerie;* Tom frequently steps outside of the action to speak to the viewers. A number of these works have clearly served to inspire Wilson: in *Our Town,* the Stage Manager acts not only as a chorus, but as a narrator and guide to the events taking place onstage. At the end of the first act, he calls an intermission, saying, "You can go out and smoke now, those that smoke."[74] In *Balm in Gilead,* Dopey turns to the audience at the conclusion of act 1, saying, "We'll call an intermission here" (act 1, p. 46); in act 2, he casually relates the background to Joe's predicament (act 2, p. 66). Similarly, at the beginning of *The Sand Castle,* Kenny faces the audience and introduces his family and, throughout the play, there are numerous incidents of this kind, including songs performed facing out from the stage.

The influence of Inge can be detected in Wilson's fondness for creating works that take place in enclosed environments. Walter Kerr described these as "snowbound":

> A "snowbound" play is any play in which a group of strangers, constituting something of a social cross-section, is forced by natural or unnatural means to remain where it is until the weather or the gunsmoke clears, by which time some or all members of the imprisoned party will have undergone character transformations.[75]

Inge's *Bus Stop* is obviously a particularly good example of this contrivance: his characters are literally "snowbound"; imprisoned in the café overnight, they are unable to leave until the bad weather has cleared. Their proximity results in all sorts of emotional and psychological upheavals and revelations, mostly predictable or maudlin. It is refreshing to note that, although Wilson may be fond of this convention, he manages to extend its possibilities. He has utilized it most notably in *Balm in Gilead, The Hotl Baltimore* and *Angels Fall*. Through firmly established dramatic parameters, he explores the complex relationships of his characters and their often witty attempts at communication. Of the last work, Gerald Weales observes that

> *Angels Fall* is another of those Wilson plays in which the dramatist brings together a disparate group of people, beset by anxiety, and allows them to talk—sometimes wittily, always articulately—while they try to cope with exterior pressures and interior doubts.[76]

Grouping Wilson with writers like Wilder and Inge is in some respects quite understandable, since all have at some time depicted small-town life and concentrated on character interaction and development. Wilson's work, however, offers a more acerbic, certainly less domestic, picture of provincial existence, the residents of his country towns usually being less innocent and more prone to venality than the sweet inhabitants of, say, *Our Town* (Martin Gottfried describes *This Is the Rill Speaking* as "a sugar-free *Our Town*"[77]) or the more knowing, though relentlessly sentimental, group in Inge's *Bus Stop*.

Wilson's manipulation of language in his rural plays recalls the work of novelists such as Willa Cather, Booth Tarkington, and Sherwood Anderson. These writers capture with accuracy and style a sense of small-town American existence. Events may seem small and even unimportant, but they develop their own resonance and, filled with portent, become consequential. Thus, what may seem trivial to those used to the cut and thrust of big-city life assumes immense importance for the inhabitants of less frenetic environments. In the main, Wilson and those who have served to inspire him are more concerned with the effect of events on the characters who people their landscapes than with the events themselves.

With this in mind, it is easy to see why Wilson's work is frequently compared with that of Chekhov; in both there is a concern for the minutiae of daily life, together with an emphasis on characters whose lives are shaped by enclosed environments, not to mention a common emphasis upon the importance of work—as in the Russian playwright's *Uncle Vanya, The Three Sisters,* and so on. Marshall Mason believes that

> Chekhov is the father of Lanford Wilson, and I see him [Wilson] as
> America's contemporary Chekhov. There is much indirect action: he
> doesn't do a lot in the way of plot. His work is nearly all character
> interaction, which is very Chekhovian.[78]

Other similarities with Chekhov exist, as Clive Barnes explains:

> What Wilson is interested in is people in transition. He has the same
> concept of change that once characterized the plays of Chekhov. His
> people are agonized, dependent, and lost in some desperation of the
> soul, but they're also people totally linked to their time and place. This
> is eventually the total link with Chekhov. . . . the comparison . . . is
> not only unmistakable but essential. [Wilson] conceives a period of
> change, at times when lives suddenly emerge and die.[79]

The Cherry Orchard's regret for time passing and fear of a new and
threatening regime is reflected, with much demotic irony, in *The
Hotl Baltimore; The Three Sisters'* dreams of escape and happiness
elsewhere find a bruising echo in practically every play Wilson has
written, from *Balm in Gilead* to *Redwood Curtain;* and the unre-
quited love in *Uncle Vanya* is given an unlikely counterpart in the
sorrows of Leslie in *The Madness of Lady Bright*.

Wilson brings honesty, compassion, and humor to everything
he writes; he is determined to express with as little falsity as possible the deepest needs of humanity and to dramatize the eternal
struggle that people endure in realizing their dreams. This drive
runs throughout his work from his earliest plays to the most recent; again and again, he slices through the defences that people
erect, through the comforts with which they surround themselves,
through their attempts at civilized living and their self-delusion
to a deeper reality beneath. Without exception, every character
that Wilson creates has a dream, and it is this dream that permits
them to function in what are, often, almost unbearably tragic cir-
cumstances.

3

Balm in Gilead

I hear America singing, the varied carols I hear—
—Walt Whitman, *Leaves of Grass*

Balm in Gilead is the earliest and perhaps most disconcerting of Wilson's urban plays. Like his other works set in a city, this drama is both ambitious and brave, seeking to cover a wide range of issues by means of unconventional, even alienating, effects. It is at once a fairly realistic chronicle of life as lived by a particular section of the New York underclass at a specific period in history and a dynamic and intensely theatrical celebration of the poetry of the streets. It deals not only with the many betrayals, disappointments, and hardships that characterize the life of its protagonists, but also with their hopes, dreams, and small victories.

The play is a coruscating, yet strangely moving evocation of a socially disadvantaged corner of New York. To become involved in its dissipated milieu is to share its fears and elations to an uncomfortable degree. Although it is set in the 1960s, with clear indications of a very "sixties" kind of mentality in its writing, it is also timeless.

Despite Wilson's concentration on the seamier elements of life, *Balm in Gilead* is far from being a depressing or unsavory work; there is much to admire, even in its bleakest moments. For example, his motley cast of characters each have the ring of absolute truth about them, and their experiences are dramatized with much knowing humor and understanding. Equally, their sometimes twisted morality is, nonetheless, rooted in a street culture that has established its own moral structure, where certain codes of conduct are permitted and others are not. Even here, certain rules may not be breached, and displays of dysfunctional (as defined by *this* society) behavior are vehemently discouraged. When the finely wrought structure is tested, discord and panic take over but, soon enough, the group reforms and the status quo is reestablished. This is nowhere more evident than in Joe's murder, which, while horrifying to all who witness it, is quickly "forgotten"—or repressed—and life continues as before.

Balm in Gilead is also extremely inventive, both in its use of language and its visual imagery. Much contrivance is at work here to ensure that word and image combine at exactly the correct moment to achieve their dramatic aim, with innovative use of lighting, repetitions both of whole scenes and snatches of dialogue, and surreal interventions by singers and children in Halloween masks all conspiring to create powerful tableaux. This is, after all, a glimpse into a world usually unseen by the majority, and Wilson takes every opportunity to mold it into a fantastic concoction of positive and negative imagery, dark and light, sound and silence, color and monochrome.

Here, for the first time, Wilson dramatizes the kindly prostitutes, losers, and frustrated dreamers who populate his other urban plays, and he indicates the direction he would take as a dramatist. In his introduction to the play, he describes those who people the work as "the riffraff, the bums, the petty thieves, the scum, the lost, the desperate, the dispossessed, the cool."[1] This may sound harsh and condemnatory, but the tone of the play is quite the opposite. At no point does he adopt a moral or censorious stance; on the contrary, his characters are delineated without apology and with considerable humor and affection.

As John Beaufort observes, "however down and out and disreputable the social castoffs of *Balm in Gilead* may be, the playwright still regards them as human beings."[2] Similarly, Gene Barnett notes that "the playwright's presentation of the characters' courage and persistence in confronting low life suggests that even such people as these have his respect."[3] Robert Brustein describes the play as basically documentary, objectively recording what Wilson observed around him; for Brustein, *Balm in Gilead* is

a closely observed sociological study of hookers, hustlers, pimps, pushers, and dopers of every sexual persuasion converging on each other in an all-night coffee shop on Halloween—Gorki's *Lower Depths* transferred to Upper Broadway.[4]

Described by John Beaufort as resembling "a verbal folk opera with set pieces for arias recited by several of its . . . characters,"[5] the action of the play takes place during the week or so prior to Halloween and spans several days. Of the thirty-two characters (including four "negro entertainers" and four children) moving in and out of the all-night café in which the work is set, the audience's attention is gradually focused on two: Joe, a dope pusher a cut above the rest of the habitués of the café in social class, and Darlene, a naive and rather stupid prostitute who has come to New York from Chicago with the intention of improving her career prospects, to become as Wilson observes, "a serious hooker."[6]

The dynamic, relentless pace suggests the kind of culture shock a young writer from Missouri must have felt when he first came to the Upper West Side of New York, finding it to be a living— albeit consumptive—museum of drugs, graffiti, and street people who seemed to exist according to their own rules. Far from feeling faint-hearted at the sights and sounds that engulfed him, Wilson seized the opportunity to become part of this counterculture.

During this period, Wilson lived in a run-down hotel named the Hebro. With two friends, he rented one large room and spent his evenings in Pan's Restaurant. Here, stunned by the diversity of life he witnessed, he eavesdropped on as many conversations as he could, becoming entranced by the street life he observed. He remembers being "so excited by the sound of what was around [him]. Those incredibly vibrant though maybe burned out lives banging against each other."[7] He elaborates:

> The night life was just so amazing to me. I made sound patterns out of what I heard and wrote down everything I heard. Every night I would just write down more and more, and anything else I heard on the street. Later, I would incorporate it all into my writing.[8]

Thus, from a back seat in a café just like the one portrayed in the play, Wilson set about watching and noting the speech and behavior of his potential cast of characters. Virtually every character in *Balm in Gilead* was inspired by someone Wilson knew during this period, and he clearly relished incorporating salient aspects of their experiences and personalities into his play, emphasizing certain areas and diminishing others.

The character of Darlene, for example, was developed from an amalgam of people he and his friends knew during their early days in New York; like them, she comes to New York from Chicago. The long description of her lining up with her "fiancé" and friends in Chicago's City Hall for a wedding licence is also based upon a real event: Wilson's friend Michael Warren Powell was at that time getting married, and underwent the same endless waiting among a similar group to those portrayed in the play (act 2, pp. 54–56).

Dopey was based on an aquaintance named Bobby, who was particularly interesting to the playwright since he "wasn't a drug addict yet, but he had *ambitions* to be an addict!"[9] Bobby actually read *Balm in Gilead,* the only one of the "cast" to do so. Wilson remembers his critique with glee: "He said, 'that's about right'. I was delighted."[10] Wilson stresses, however, that Dopey's speeches are not verbatim representations of Bobby's, observing that "if Bobby had said those things, I believe that's how he would have said them."[11] Similarly, Michael Warren Powell, the first actor to play the character, notes that, "while Lanford put the words in Dopey's mouth, they were not foreign."[12]

Powell knew Bobby—and many of the other characters in the play—very well indeed. With Wilson, he lived among them, becoming familiar with their physical demeanor and speech rhythms. Taking on the part of Dopey therefore evolved almost by osmosis, with director Marshall Mason encouraging his cast to closely identify with their roles. Powell recalls:

> Marshall was at the time very into Stanislavski and so we virtually lived the roles for the whole rehearsal period. We used to hang out in a place very similar to the one Lanford had written about [the original café, Pan's, was no longer in existence] whose clièntele was almost identical. Rehearsals were invariably set for midnight and so the lateness of the hour added its own dimension.[13]

While Dopey's speeches are fictionalized versions of their original's discourse, the monologue spoken by Fick at the end of act 1 was reproduced virtually verbatim. Fick is based upon a "tiny, stringy little guy"[14] Wilson encountered early one morning:

> Fick's character evolved out of an experience that occurred during a driving thunderstorm at 3 o'clock in the morning. I came out of

the 72nd Street subway stop, and this guy latched onto me and ran backwards beside me all the way to the hotel door. I told him, "I'm really very sorry, I just don't have a nickel for you." It wasn't what he had asked for at all. He just wanted to talk. You know, "If I had a buddy, if I just had somebody I could pass down the street with." Just company.[15]

In the play, Fick's need to pass the time with someone is explained still further. He states: "See I'm on *H* [heroin], I mean, I'm flying and I gotta talk man" (act 1, p. 45). After the above episode, Wilson went straight back to his hotel room and wrote down everything the man had said to him: "I had never heard anything like it," he recalls, "as a result, almost the entire part of Fick was written in one sitting. This guy was one of those people who spoke in poetry, so foreign; such a strange style and with a wonderful mix of dialects."[16] Elsewhere, he notes that the whole episode was "an exercise in getting down exactly what he said, exactly the way he said it."[17]

At the time he wrote *Balm in Gilead,* Wilson recalls that he had an almost perfect ear; he could reproduce conversations—and written matter—almost verbatim as much as two years later. Wilson confirms that "a lot of the play is dictation . . . I was just trying to take things I'd heard and adapt them to a flow."[18] Until then, he had not realized that he had a natural talent for accurately reproducing dialogue with all of its verbal idiosyncrasies and repetitions:

> I didn't realize it until I started writing plays. . . . Not only do I hear the way people talk—and the specific rhythms of their speech—but I have a talent for reproducing that in an organized and exciting way. *That* is a talent—everything else is work.[19]

Balm in Gilead was originally conceived by Wilson as a novel, and some time elapsed before he revised his manuscript into a play format. Never believing for a moment that it could ever be produced (in the first draft, a total of fifty-five characters were included; he would later amalgamate some of them and eliminate others), Wilson felt completely unrestricted and thoroughly immersed himself in experimentation. The scope and breadth of the work allowed Wilson to experiment on a scale he had never previously imagined, and a number of the theatrical devices that would later become his trademarks were incorporated: the mesmerizing, confusing, overlapping dialogue with several characters conversing simultaneously; direct audience address; innovative use of staging techniques and lighting, together with a musicality bordering on the operatic. He recalls:

> I never believed it could be produced so it didn't matter what I did. I included everything in sight . . . and, of course we were going to see many wonderfully experimental works, and much of the play is clearly taken from other things. Much of it isn't; much of it is totally original, but I did absorb a *lot* of other influences.[20]

Joan Littlewood's Chicago production of *The Hostage* was a direct influence, and there are clear indications of the impact on Wilson of such works as Maxim Gorki's *The Lower Depths* and Eugene O'Neill's *The Iceman Cometh*. The play's circularity of form owes much to a work by Gertrude Stein, *In Circles*, which Wilson saw at the Judson Poets Theatre. Equally, Wilson states his piece was influenced by an experimental dance group who were working in the same theatre at the time. He recalls how emotionally affected he was by the dance:

> It was set in the middle of a big, open stage and, in the middle, the cast moved the piano across the stage while the pianist was still playing. Later, very gradually, they slid the piano back over to where it originally was. . . . moving that piano was just one of the most moving moments I had ever seen. I didn't know what it meant, but it was terrific! So the moving of the set around in a circle that occurs in *Balm in Gilead* was directly influenced by that.[21]

The moving of the set has been attempted only once, and that was in the first production of the piece; the subsequent revivals directed by John Malkovich have not repeated the process. Wilson regrets this, although he acknowledges that the Malkovich productions were extremely effective. Ideally, however, he believes that the work benefits from this visual counterpoint to its circularity:

> Virtually the whole set turns inside out. . . . I couldn't do it without it meaning something; the whole play is written in little circles, all

contributing to and commenting upon the overall structure. . . . Even
the monologues spin back on themselves, turning in circles.[22]

Wilson describes the physical action of the play thus:

> Everything seems to move in a circle. Within the general large pattern
> the people who spend their nights at the café have separate goals and
> separate characters but together they constitute a whole, revolving
> around some common center.[23]

An excellent example of Wilson's use of the circular motif occurs immediately prior to Joe's murder. John cries to the children
who have recently appeared onstage in Halloween masks: "Go on,
scram. Get out of here. Scram out of here. Go on!" (act 2, p. 68)
The lights dim, and the Stranger stabs Joe "underhanded in the
heart"[24] as the children run out, not understanding, "screaming
and yelling joyously."[25] To add to the nightmarish and surreal
aura onstage, they immediately return after circling the café set,
entering from the back and running through again. Exactly the
same scene is repeated, though this time the children flee screaming in terror. The chilling atmosphere of unreality is compounded
by Wilson's instruction that, following the murder, "There is a time
lapse. No one mentions the stabbing."[26] Life continues as though
nothing has happened.

In his production notes, Wilson states that much of the play
"consists of simultaneous conversations in various groups with
dialogue either overlapping or interlocking. These sections should
flow as a whole, without specific focus; they rise and subside and
scenes develop from them."[27] Later, he indicates that "each group,
and there are several of them, must maintain a kind of life of
its own. . . . Improvised, unheard conversations may be used. . . .
Their lines should come from scenes developed within the situation."[28]

The characters themselves sometimes become a living part of
the café set, as when they "stand in a line across stage, back to the
audience, forming a 'wall.' There is a space about four feet wide
at the center of the wall, forming a doorway. Joe and Darlene walk
down the wall slowly."[29] Similarly, a mesmeric visual counterpoint
to any changes onstage occurs every time a new character arrives.
Wilson describes how

everyone in the café (with the exception of Babe and Fick) looks up the moment someone enters . . . a kind of reflex "once-over" to evaluate any new opportunity or threat.[30]

Balm in Gilead is clearly the work of a young and headstrong dramatist; any flaws it may have arise out of an urgent need to experiment with the technical possibilities of theatre. Marshall Mason has commented both on the tremendous vitality that imbues the text and on the clear indication that Wilson was a playwright with great natural potential. Wilson was, however, still learning at this stage and was keen to expand his skills. Mason observes that

[Wilson's] early writing had great originality and energy, but he wanted to grow as a playwright, particularly in terms of learning structure. . . . [His work is] structured by its inner drive, which is almost like music.[31]

Further, Mason notes that Wilson incorporates such poetry, combined with the most naturalistic sounds, to achieve his aim:

There is a great energy in the play; it's teeming with naturalistic life, but at the same time [Wilson] was also experimenting with the here and now of the theatre in a very vivid present-tense kind of way. He much admires the work of Brendan Behan, and *Balm in Gilead* has a similarly vivid use of language.[32]

Wilson's extraordinarily inventive manipulation of language, particularly "street" and debased language, is here already resoundingly in evidence. His abilities as a poet are also developing, although there are occasions when the music of language is rendered in a somewhat obvious and strained fashion, and can sound a little false and self-conscious. One example occurs when several people order coffee at the same time:

Ernesto. Just the coffee's okay. Black. Black.
Ann. Black.
John. Black.
Joe. Look! (act 1, p. 14)

Although this bears rather obvious hallmarks of "artistic" contrivance and poeticizing, these *were* very early days in Wilson's writing career. What is remarkable is that the vast majority of the poetry in the play is seamless, sophisticated, and complex enough to bear close scrutiny and analysis.

Wilson's use of alliteration and assonance frequently recalls works such as Dylan Thomas's *Under Milk Wood,* where disparate snippets of dialogue eventually cohere into a mosaic of meaning. In *Balm in Gilead,* the sounds produced by various characters create an aural miasma of interlocking and overlapping noises. This is very strong in the opening moments of the play, when the bustle and raucousness of street life are forcefully implied:

Tig. [*overlapping*] What are you, some kind of housewife, Judy?
Judy. [*to* DAVID] You're the housewife, aren't you, sweetheart?
David. You're the fishwife, Judy. Fishwife, Fish. Pheew! (act 1, p. 7)

This and other conversations are repeated in the second act (act 2, p. 64), where the echoing of the words provides a hypnotic counterpoint to the vaguely drug-induced euphoria evident onstage. These repetitions are a source of confusion even to some of the characters; after listening to a series of conversations identical to those in the first act and then being informed that Joe is about to be murdered, the drug-addled Fick is completely nonplused. He asks "We ain't seen this, have we?" (act 2, p. 67).

Repetitions and circularity of theme also mark the hard, consonantal sounds that reverberate and twang throughout the work and establish an impression both of speed and of harsh, soulless interactions. At one point, Ann states, "He don't truck with that junk. He'd better not; I'd crack him over the head" (act 1, p. 11); and at another, Tim says, "At least I'm drunk on drunk, not on junk like everyone" (act 1, p. 17). The slang of the streets has permeated the diction of Wilson's characters as surely as the air they breathe; its jazzlike rhythms infect almost every word they speak. For example, Fick describes how he has been beaten up: "I tell you they had me pinned, man. Down in this hall-thing. Four or five big black cats, they must have been huge" (act 1, p. 43); and Judy indicates her jealousy over Rust's relationship with Terry: "You sawed-of [*sic*] little bitch, you moving in? You moving into our pad. . . . Get your hot little ass out of here, now." (act 1, p. 31).

The repeated use of slang unites them, no matter how aggressive or violent the content of their speech; their knowledge and use of such argot forms a bond that allows them to function, to operate, apart from mainstream society. Delighting in the use of the expletives that pepper their conversation, they exclude the faint-hearted, who would find it impossible to cope with such a hostile and challenging atmosphere; these are mean, tough streets, and the only way to survive is to adopt a hard veneer, both verbal and physical.

The jargon used by drug addicts and other hustlers is also closely observed; the reluctant drug-pusher, Joe, expresses his distaste for the cattle syringe the Stranger takes from his pocket: "You don't use something like that. That's too fancy. You use a works. An eye dropper, a piece of dollar. A needle." (act 2, p. 67). At the foot of the page on which this text appears, Wilson explains that "a junkie seldom uses a syringe. He uses an eye-dropper, attached to a surgical needle with a thin piece of paper rolled around the needle, serving as a gasket. For paper they often use a thin strip torn from the edge of a dollar bill."

Elsewhere, the character's use of nonsense language also takes on a jargonized tone; although one may be little wiser when confronted cold with the actual words, in the context of performance the mystery unravels itself. A good example occurs during a brief contretemps between the drunken Tim and Judy (a lesbian); Judy tries to help get Tim home, but he misconstrues her concern and calls her "a whatsit," turning to the audience as if to explain: "She's a whatsit, without a gizmo" (act 1, p. 17).

Wilson's use of language, dazzling throughout the work, is perhaps at its most impressive in a number of superbly timed and controled monologues that appear at fairly regular intervals. The playwright's talent for such writing is at its best in this play. Of particular note are those spoken by Dopey, by Fick, and, especially, by Darlene. Her long and discursive monologue was originally intended by Wilson to be a short story but, he recalls, "about half-way through the writing of it, I decided it was going to be in the play."[33] At first, Wilson intended it to comprise the entire second act; originally written to last forty-five minutes, it now runs for about twenty-six minutes.

John Malkovich has hailed this speech as containing "arguably some of the best writing of the last 40 to 50 years."[34] For him, Darlene forms the centerpiece of the play, which he sees as being essentially about "a girl who comes to the big city. A very dumb, dumb girl who is really pretty pathetic and sad."[35]

Without once descending into parody or adopting a patronizing tone, Wilson expertly guides and delineates Darlene's rambling, frequently incoherent, thoughts. He describes her character as "not at all bright. . . . she is supposed to be stupid, and not the sweet, girl-next-door, common-sense-saves-the-day type of inge- nue."[36] Wilson's attitude toward Darlene might seem to be rather harsh; although he clearly feels affection for her, he nonetheless uncompromisingly conveys her innate stupidity and vulnerability, not least by the absurdity of her explanation to Ann that an albino is "a kind of horse" (act 2, p. 53), as she tries to describe a for- mer lover.

Darlene tells a story that is absolutely believable without any prettifying of its basic sadness or any attempt to make it more interesting. She is without the sophistication that might prompt her to at least partially rewrite her (not very thrilling) history for the benefit of the listener. Like the truly ingenuous, she be- lieves her story to be fascinating and rambles on endlessly. It is, on the surface at least, tedious, repetitive, pathetic, and appar- ently pointless.

Darlene buttonholes Ann and offers vague recollections inar- ticulately—and very probably inaccurately—delivered. In ver- balizing her memories, she reveals herself with total and poignant candour, mercilessly signalling her flaws and weaknesses and un- selfconsciously conveying her credulity and stupidity.

Wilson thus portrays Darlene as a disappointed fantastist who clings to muddled dreams of love and old romances. So vague is her recollection of the good times that, when she tries to reclaim a memory of a comforting experience from the past, she inadvert- ently relays a tale of ineffable sadness. Unable to recall the name of the park near her Chicago apartment or the name of the hotel from which her favorite "collected" towel came, she attempts to describe for Ann something of her "love affair" with Cotton:

Darlene. . . . Old Cotton had, I'll swear, the funniest temperament I ever saw. If he got mad . . . he wouldn't argue or anything like that, he'd just walk around like nothing was wrong only never say one word. . . . Course I make it sound worse than it was, cause he didn't act like that very often. Fortunately. But you never knew what was

> going to provoke him, I swear. . . . And when we decided to get
> married all our friends were so excited—of course, they'd been ex-
> pecting it probably. But we were so crazy you'd never know what we
> were going to do. I know he used to set the TV so it pointed into
> the mirror, because there wasn't a plug-in by the bed and we'd lay
> there in bed and look at the mirror that had the TV reflected in it.
> Only everything was backwards. Writing was backwards. . . . Only,
> you know, even backwards, it was a better picture, it was clearer than
> if you was just looking straight at it. (act 2, pp. 52–53)

Darlene's monologue has all the hallmarks of real speech, full of
ellipses, pauses, and non sequiturs. Wilson draws on her inarticulateness to delineate character at the same time as he seamlessly
suggests her nostalgic longing for the past and her need for such
reminiscence. It is what sustains her. In this respect, she is like all
the other lonely and emotionally hungry people in the café—
indeed, in Wilson's urban plays; she needs to talk, to have someone
listen to her, and she wants to hold on to a rapidly disintegrating
past that daily seems to move further away. To speak the words
aloud somehow helps to make them true.

The anecdote is given added authenticity by Darlene's frequent
use of interjections such as "I'll swear," "of course," and "you
know." And, despite her verbal stumblings, she obviously enjoys
telling her story; her eagerness to relive what must have been,
ironically, the happiest period of her life is forcefully conveyed.

Wilson's overt use of poetic imagery and heightened language
is noticeable here. Poetry and practicality combine to achieve the
desired effect: because of the lack of a plug by the bed, Cotton
turned the television so that its image was reflected in the mirror.
What is ostensibly a very mundane and ordinary action is here
given immense depth. Everything that Darlene and Cotton
watched on television was seen backwards; the resulting imperfect
image was, nonetheless, considered by Darlene to be "a better
picture . . . clearer than if you was just looking straight at it." This
clearly has implications far beyond the prosaic: Darlene prefers
to regard life at an oblique angle, hoping that the view she is
granted will be an improvement on a more cruel and harsh reality.

Darlene's fundamental dimness is skillfully woven into the fabric of her speech; by qualifying many of her apparently factual
statements, she deflates or undermines her most heartfelt sentiments. Realizing that her description of Cotton's tendency to

mope about in silence for days on end may make him sound unattractive or undesirable to her audience, she suddenly inter- jects that she is exaggerating, making his behavior "sound worse than it was, cause he didn't act like that very often. Fortunately." Similarly, when she and Cotton had finally decided to marry, she gleefully exclaims that their friends were "so excited" for them, but her joy is immediately diminished as she adds "of course, they'd been expecting it probably."

By such subtle linguistic means, Wilson illuminates Darlene's complexity, while simultaneously demonstrating, once again, his profoundly humane attitude toward those he dramatizes. It is all too easy to reject such a character out of hand and to become impatient with her dizziness and self-delusion, but, in Wilson's hands, Darlene's very inarticulateness speaks volumes about her plight and reminds us that no one's experiences are worthless or simplistic.

Dopey is described by Wilson as "a heroin addict as well as a sometimes-not-too-good hustler."[37] With little to recommend him for it, this character has nonetheless adopted the role of commen- tator on the action for the benefit of the audience. He is one of those characters who can frequently be found on park benches, who will engage one in interminable expositions of his opinions on the world and its problems; an ersatz philosopher, he airs his views or attempts to clarify—often where no clarification is required—any issue that comes to mind.

Throughout act 1, Dopey's ramblings serve as a verbal backdrop to onstage events. In the first section of his long speech, he labori- ously explains what he sees as the workings of the pimp-and- prostitute relationship; later, he stresses his concern over the resil- ience of cockroaches. In his mind, the two subjects would seem to be inextricably linked. Wilson indicates that the following part of Dopey's monologue should be spoken as though he were "a bit irritated":[38]

> *Dopey.* . . . it's a crawling bughouse up there. . . . all the roaches play- ing like games on the floor. . . . A roach's *attitude* just gripes the hell out of me. But what burns me, I've been reading up, not re- cently. . . . they [were] around about two million years before man, you know, before we came along: Anthropologists or whatever, ge- ologists over in Egypt or somewhere, looking for the first city, they

dug down through a city, and straight on down through another, you know, they're piled up like a sandwich or in layers like a seven-layer cake. . . . But not only that! They've made tests, and they found out that a roach can stand—if there was going to be a big atom explosion, they can stand something like *fourteen times* as much radio-whatever-it-is, you-know-activity as we can. So after every man, woman, and child is wiped out and gone, like you imagine, those same goddamn cockroaches will be still crawling around happy as you please over the ruins of everything. Now the picture of that really gripes my ass. (act 1, pp. 26–27)

Dopey adopts a confiding tone and prattles on as though he were an authority on the life expectancy of cockroaches, although he is almost certainly merely resurrecting half-forgotten facts from the hinterland of his atrophied brain. In a misguided attempt to back up his statements with a little learning and objective proof, he states that he has been "reading up, not recently" on the evolution of the insects. Just how seriously we are meant to take this assertion is unclear.

Dopey's use of language nicely complements the disarray of his ideas: he interrupts his sentences with endless commas and repetitions of "you know" and "like," his muddle-headedness even extends to forgetting the correct word for radioactivity and then punctuating his groping with "whatever-it-is" and, again, "you know".

The longevity and resilience of cockroaches clearly annoys Dopey; their hardiness is an affront to someone whose daily existence is fraught with precarious health problems and the fiscal dangers inherent in drug addiction. About as far down the social scale as it is possible to drop, Dopey nonetheless steadfastly classes himself with the rest of humanity and misses the irony implicit in his opinions. Disgusted with and dismissive of what he believes to be a particularly revolting form of insect life, he nonetheless personally enacts a lifestyle not entirely dissimilar to such creatures by foraging, scavenging, and living in whichever corner he can find.

That the cockroach can, apparently, withstand almost any form of attack, even nuclear, is very telling: in one form or another, people like Dopey manage to survive despite incredible odds. They exist in the most abject poverty, withstand disease and infection, and even manage to escape those who would destroy or restrict them. Metaphorical deinfestation may periodically occur, but some members of the attacked always survive.

Unknowingly lending weight to the connection between certain sections of humanity and cockroaches, Dopey anthropomorphizes the insects, calling their "attitude" unacceptable. To illustrate his skewed point of view, he attributes human characteristics to their antics wherever possible: "playing like games on the floor"; "crawling around happy as you please."

Fick is another drug addict who shares something of Dopey's predilection for constant chatter. He will, according to Wilson, "talk to anything that moves,"[39] and so the long monologue toward the end of act 1 is merely an extension of an interminable and garbled diatribe, full of woeful self-pity, that has continued for some time. Fick variously complains of the cold, of becoming ill (he explains that he is "weak as a kitten" (act 1, p. 44) due to his heroin addiction that began when he was only thirteen), of not having anyone to talk to, and, particularly, of needing protection. The speech reaches its climax when he describes how "four or five big black cats. . . . big, strong fellows" have beaten him up:

> *Fick.* . . . And they pushed me into this alley, not an alley, but this hallway and back down the end of that to this dark place at the end of the hallway and they start punching at me, and I just fell into this ball on the floor so they couldn't hurt me or nothing. But if I came down there with a couple of fighters, a couple of guys, like my friends, it wouldn't have to be you or anything, but just a couple or three guys, big guys, like walking down the street, you know. . . . just a few guys and they'd leave me be, maybe, because they'd think I had these buddies that looked after me, you know . . . (act 1, p. 45)

The long first sentence, interrupted by only three commas, forcefully suggests a succession of muddled thoughts and half-forgotten memories; as these swim and curve through Fick's mind, Wilson implies the speech rhythms of one whose mental state owes much to a chemically induced euphoria. To Fick, all dark places seem the same; in his desperation to remember the "facts" of the attack on him, he confuses the location, first stating that it took place in an alley and then immediately retracting this in favor of a hallway.

While there is much bleak humor in Wilson's treatment of the plight of Fick, whose paranoid repetitions and panicky tone accurately portray the kind of chaotic discourse associated with addicts and alcoholics, there is also pathos and compassion.

Fick casts around for an inordinate amount of time in an effort to harness attention and assistance from someone, anyone; he desperately tries to advertize his predicament without actually addressing any particular individual. For him, the possibility of rejection is too strong; it is easier to talk generally and without specific focus. Fick knows that his companions' perception of him is negative in the extreme; on their list of those deserving of assistance and friendship, he ranks very low.

It is highly unlikely that any of Fick's companions in the café will help him; they have problems enough of their own. Even if they do not consider themselves to be leading dysfunctional lives—which is possible for some of the more vague inhabitants—they are almost certainly too lazy or apathetic to care or to become involved. For others, life is already hard enough, fraught with danger and uncertainty; taking responsibility for and protecting themselves is a full-time job.

It is therefore all the more pathetic that Fick should try to suggest that he is among friends. Although he specifies that his proposed helpers should be "fighters," "friends," and "big guys," he dare not point to anyone in particular. People stand up and move away, but still Fick keeps on talking, in the hope that eventually a kindly soul will take pity on him and take his part.

Besides the usually jagged and discordant music in the speech rhythms of its characters, there is also a great deal of actual music in the play, signalling the constant noise and bustle of city life. Here, silence is a very rare commodity. To illustrate this, the opening moments of the play are described as follows:

> A noise from a crowd begins and reaches a peak as the curtain rises. From the wings come four Negro entertainers (two from each side) who sing a rock'n'roll song with much clapping, dancing, etc. They are accompanied by a typical clangy, catchy instrumentation. From far out on the apron they sing to the audience—very animated. As the song fades out, and they begin to move (still singing) back off the stage, the noise from the group rises again.[40]

Thus, music permeates the entire fabric of *Balm in Gilead:* during a rare calm moment, John observes that "When it gets quiet in here you almost think something's gonna happen" (act 1, p. 20), and the quartet of black singers starts up a "soft blues";[41] Rake and Ernesto add to the overall circularity of the piece with their "round" song entitled "Men on the Corner," the melody of which Wilson describes as "shockingly gentle; rocking; easy; soft; lilting."[42] This song requires that all participants sing a line each, taking turns; Rake encourages his friends to join in by singing the song through himself:

> They laugh and jab
> cavort and jump
> and joke and gab
> and grind and bump.
>
> They flip a knife
> and toss a coin
> and spend their life
> and scratch their groin.
>
> They pantomime
> a standing screw
> and pass the time
> with nought to do.
>
> They swing, they sway
> this cheerful crew,
> with nought to say
> and nought to do. (act 1, p. 41)

To further the incessant musicality, Wilson also provides the music for this song (act 1, p. 41). Later, the concluding moments of Darlene's long monologue are accompanied by the quartet as they "harmonize in a rock'n'roll wordless 'Boo, bop, boo, bah, day, dolie, olie day' kind of rambling that gets louder and eventually takes over the scene."[43] Later, they sing a jazzed up version of the famous hymn "There Is a Balm in Gilead,", which has provided the title of the play. The play concludes with another rendition of the "round" song, but this time performed "not as a round, but [with the cast] all singing softly and liltingly."[44]

Wilson had a strong religious upbringing, and theological argument and imagery recur throughout his work (notably in *Bron-*

tosaurus and *Angels Fall*). Indeed, he refers to his plays as "Baptist sermons,"[45] whose purpose is to question behavior and motivation.

Of all Wilson's dramas, *Balm in Gilead* is perhaps the most deeply saturated with religion. Its monologues often resemble corrupt sermons; actions are repeated, giving an impression of iconographic imagery; music takes on a ritualistic, celebratory function; and the setting of the work echoes a city of lost souls akin to Sodom and Gomorrah. However, the only reference to any kind of balm in the play occurs during a conversation between Tig and Ernesto (act 1, p. 20) when they discuss the ancient rituals of the Egyptians.

In the Old Testament, Gilead is the name of both Manasseh's grandson and a historic mountainous region east of the River Jordan. Wilson uses the latter as a "type" for his play: in the books of Genesis and Jeremiah, Gilead is cited as being famous for its medicinal balm,[46] although, in Hosea, it is described as "the iniquity of Gilead" and as "a city of evil doers, tracked with blood."[47] Yet another reference occurs in the book of Samuel, where it is noted that some of the Hebrews took refuge in Gilead to avoid the ravages of the Philistines.[48]

There are clear analogies to be made with contemporary New York and an earlier city of "iniquity" and of "evil doers", not to mention a city of the disenfranchised clinging together and seeking refuge and comfort—or a soothing balm—away from the marauding and cut-throat city outside. As John Beaufort notes, "the irony of the title remains that there is no balm in this Manhattan Gilead. There is instead the vulnerable companionship of outcasts, destructive delusion of drugs, and pursuit of sordid pleasures."[49]

It is noteworthy that Margaret Atwood's futuristic novel, *The Handmaid's Tale* (1987) is set in a late-twentieth century Monotheocracy named Gilead, whose spurious history is the subject of the Symposium reported at the conclusion of the novel. The audience is exhorted by the speaker to recall that Gileadean society was under a great deal of pressure and that therefore caution must be exercised in "passing moral judgement"[50] on it.

Balm in Gilead is one of Wilson's most successful and critically acclaimed works. Since its premiere, it has enjoyed a high reputation among critics and audiences alike; it is a play that thrives on repetitions, counterpoints, and juxtapositions and that often seems to work in spite of itself. Sometimes *so* much is happening at once that confusion is a distinct possibility; that this is never realized testifies to Wilson's discipline as a dramatist.

For all the play's visual brilliance, for me its greatest strength resides in its manipulation of language. Wilson's ability to mold shards of street language into a kind of vibrant *vers libre* is first revealed here. Even the dim-witted Darlene's shaky grasp of story-telling is elevated into something profound and moving, and Dopey's and Fick's hallucinatory ramblings become far more than mundane and pointless verbiage. Much later, dramatists such as Sam Shepard and David Mamet were also to create poetry out of the basest forms of speech but, as early as 1964, Wilson's was the pioneering achievement in this area.

4

The Hotl Baltimore

All things change

—Heraclitus

The Hotl Baltimore is Wilson's valedictory poem for a lost world. He has stated that the play is compilation of "all the damn rooming houses and hotels [he] had lived in,"[1] but it is far more than a mere documentary recreation of experience. Here, he paints a picture of good things gone to seed, of a gradual falling away of standards. His description of the set of the condemned hotel lobby adds to the vaguely surreal air of the proceedings and is clearly intended to act as a constant visual counterpoint to the developing action:

> The lobby is represented by three areas that rise as the remains of a building already largely demolished: the Front Desk, the lounge, and the stairway.[2]

Through the metaphor of a moribund but once glamorous hotel, Wilson explores the decline of urban America, the gradual decimation of old-fashioned values like neighborliness and fraternity, the consequent breakdown in communication and understanding among individuals, and, as the residents move on to other lives, even the gradual dissolution of family life.

Just as *Balm in Gilead* demonstrated Wilson's ability to dramatize widely diverging themes within a tightly controlled pattern of events, so *The Hotl Baltimore* permits him to deal with universal issues within a tiny spatial framework.

Writing a play around the idea of the deterioration of the cities

80

had interested Wilson for some time. In 1980, he observed that "we change so quickly, we in America. I guess I might be saying something like, 'look at what you're throwing away before you throw it away.'"[3] The crumbling Hotel itself and, indeed, a number of its inhabitants, are on their last legs; relics from a bygone era, they crave support in a rapidly changing world. They may be seriously weakened and broken down, but, in order to shore up strength against what he sees as the deleterious onslaught of crass modernism upon society, Wilson suggests that they are well worth saving and preserving.

Writing specifically about *The Madness of Lady Bright*, the *Fifth of July* and, particularly, *The Hotl Baltimore*, Michiko Kakutani has observed that

> what [Wilson's] disparate characters all share is a peculiarly American sense of dislocation, a sense of having lost connection with their pasts. Haunted by memories of how things used to be, these characters spend their days searching after their misplaced dreams, and they talk nostalgically of the time when "everything was an event."[4]

To compound the overall sense of disruption and etiolation in the play, many of the characters' experiences similarly reflect instability. Wilson therefore includes people whose minds are vaguely unhinged, their imaginations spurred by past events rather than current issues. Both Millie and Mr. Morse exemplify this tendency. Wilson's passion for dramatizing those with unconventional lifestyles follows on quite naturally from this; his characters include the familiar quota of feisty prostitutes whose uneasy acceptance of their lot is forever on the verge of revolt and whose humor propels the action; of disenchanted lovers, and of outcasts and drifters whose desperate need to belong to society usually backfires.

Despite some similarities in the type of characters portrayed and the fact that their small, yet persistent dreams make up a good part of the play, the world portrayed by Wilson in *The Hotl Baltimore* is nevertheless a very long way from *Balm in Gilead*. Those in the later play may also be frayed around the edges and in urgent need of support, but the majority also exhibit a marked degree of empathy and optimism not immediately evident in most of their earlier, street-hardened counterparts. They seem kinder, more selfless and, despite their relative poverty and low position in society, more dignified. This is perhaps in part due to their physical location; rather than conducting their affairs on the streets and cafés of a run-down section of the city, this group has at least managed to secure a home base of sorts that, for all its inadequacies, is at least a shelter. People actually *live* here, as opposed to merely passing through en route to other destinations (although there is indeed a keen sense of transience in these tenancies).

In turn, this permits them to establish an improved version of the kind of "family" group depicted in the earlier play. The familial undertow is reinforced since those onstage represent varying generations from grandparents to recalcitrant teenagers, with ersatz parents and children interacting or conflicting according to their moods.

As ever, the majority of Wilson's characters display lovable personality traits; their eccentricities and idiosyncrasies contribute to superbly rounded characterizations. Richard Watts describes them as "friendly people, though a little crazy ... [whose] thoughts, woes, confidences and self-revelations make an engaging and sympathetic play,"[5] while for Jack Kroll they are "the beautiful losers—the deadbeats, walking wounded, crippled-up-the-creekers, along with their inevitable muse, the golden whore."[6]

Wilson seizes every opportunity to milk the all-pervading nostalgia for all it is worth; he delights in peppering the work with comforting home-spun homilies, old-fashioned value judgments, and appeals for a nicer, saner world. Even the younger characters are filled with a longing for better times; while dreaming of the future, they also look back to the past.

The playwright's philosophy is exemplified in the play's principal character, the Girl, a young prostitute who acts as a spokesperson for Wilson's own views; the writer has confirmed that she "has a lot of [himself] in her."[7] She is forever reflecting that things are no longer what they were. For example, in days gone by, she had felt a sense of community with the passengers on the trains that passed her home, but now these days and all corresponding associations have disappeared:

> *Girl.* I never waved to a single person who didn't wave back to me. If
> you saw something important to you neglected. . . . They've let the

roadbeds go to hell. You have to close your eyes on a train. Or look out the window. That's still beautiful; some of it. In the country. (act 1, p. 20)

A little earlier, confronted with a picture from the "grand opening" of the hotel, she had observed how the hotel now "looks just like it used to, only dirty" (act 1, p. 11). She could be talking about her life experiences and those of her companions onstage.

Like *Balm in Gilead*, *The Hotl Baltimore* relies more on character interaction than plot development. Such works tend, as Harold Branam observes, to be "uneven, diffuse, almost plotless, with the subject matter providing the main interest."[8] Here, a group of disparate characters are brought together "in an interesting setting (usually threatened, usually around a holiday)"[9]—in this case the lobby of a soon-to-be demolished hotel, on "a recent Memorial Day,"[10] the experiences of its characters being followed from 7:30 in the morning until after midnight.

The action arises not from the kind of major emotional or psychological traumas that can be found in the likes of *Heartbreak House, Night of the Iguana*, or even *Grand Hotel* (which, on a superficial level at least, share a roughly similar setting and deal with issues arising from their mismatched characters' propinquity) but from routine, even banal, encounters. This is an everyday world, peopled with the flotsam and jetsam of society. As the characters pass in and out of the lobby, their entrances and exits provide counterpoints of conflict and, while failing to provide a linear thread, are interesting events in themselves.

For example, Mr. Morse and Jamie engage in an impotent squabble about their game of checkers; Jackie tries to convince someone to lend his signature to some dubious paperwork; she later finds that a piece of land she has purchased in Utah (via a radio advertisement) is completely worthless, and the Girl tries to help everyone she sees in any way she can. The whores and their "johns" come and go, cracking sardonic jokes and complaining about their lot. Eventually, Jackie abandons her slow-witted brother, Jamie, who is last seen dancing in the lobby with the warm-hearted April. The montage of effects depicts humanity's ability to continue to hope in a spiritually desolate world. The play is therefore structured through an accumulation of linked events; what at first seems random and haphazard gradually becomes integrated into the fabric of the work as a whole. The audience is subliminally seduced into involvement until, as Mel Gussow has noted, "we feel the pace of the hotel and the pulse of the characters."[11]

To illustrate Wilson's sense of timing and structure, it is instructive to look at one of the set pieces he develops in the play that gain their power from a sense of accumulation: the series of events leading to the conclusion of the first act constitutes a model of contrivance and theatrical bravura.

As Mr. Morse's cantankerous complaints, Jackie's aggressive tirades, and the arguments among April and Mr. Katz and Bill and the Girl build to a crescendo, Suzy suddenly appears wearing nothing but a towel. Total mayhem ensues, with recriminations and insults ricocheting around the stage; Bill turns on the radio to add to the confusion and din. As a lunatic counterpoint to all of this, Mr. Morse "begins to march up and down swinging the barbells"[12] and embarks on an apparently endless rendition of "O sole mio."[13] The act ends with Jamie's entrance:

> Jamie carries a box down the stairs, dropping it when he sees the naked Suzy. Staring with his mouth open. The box contains hotel soap, towels, washcloths, etc., and things stolen from the neighborhood shops. Nearly everyone on stage laughs as Jamie gapes at Suzy and the lights fade. The music soars over their laughter.[14]

In this final, frozen image, Wilson neatly encapsulates what is fundamental about the play: innocence and humor (Jamie's childishness and naiveté as he stands dumbstruck at the sight of Suzy's nakedness—perhaps the first time he has ever seen a woman in such a state); petty criminality and pathos (the fallen box containing a vaguely pathetic booty signals the modest aspirations of those who would bother to steal it—it may not add up to much, but at least it represents some kind of material accumulation); and love and tolerance (the genuinely affectionate, if raucous, laughter that rings out indicates the empathy "nearly everyone onstage" feels with Jamie's plight. It is a tableau almost cinematic in design, while at the same time recalling a particularly demotic version of the "stage pictures"—contrived, artistically-structured images—so favored in the drama of W. B. Yeats.

Not only is every physical interaction minutely orchestrated, but

Wilson's manipulation of language is correspondingly meticulous, with meandering dialogue taking on an almost musical rhythm. He utilizes to the full the melodic potential of the many unfinished and overlapping speeches and melds them into a complex mesh of rhythms and cadences. Director Marshall Mason notes:

> Both in terms of its language and its action, *The Hotl Baltimore* is a refinement of what Lanford had unearthed in *Balm in Gilead;* the technique has now become so fine—and fully integrated into both the action and the characters—that the music of language is virtually hidden; you are unaware that he is poeticizing and it seems, on the surface, to be very, very realistic. It is, of course, far from it: directing it, I found that every move had been minutely planned, every development meticulously set up, and the words the characters spoke were pure poetry.[15]

Compared with the experimental vigor informing every scene of *Balm in Gilead,* Wilson's concept and staging of *The Hot Baltimore* is conventional, "well-made," even traditional in nature; it marks a return to old-fashioned and therefore perhaps unfashionable ideas—particularly in the early 1970s, when cynicism, even nihilism, seemed to be the order of the day. Wilson even surprised himself; describing the intuitive origins of the work and how he almost imperceptibly moved away from the mosaic impressionism of his earlier plays, he observes that:

> I thought it would be a montage like *Balm in Gilead* or *The Rimers of Eldritch,* that it would not be realistic, and that the characters would go out to the street and up to their rooms. But I was writing very fast and characters kept coming into the play, most of them based on the people I knew. I thought, apparently we're going to stay in the lobby.[16]

Jack Kroll applauds Wilson's courage in producing a play so much at odds with contemporary thinking, calling it "daring" and observing that the work is "so old-fashioned in its humanity that it's the freshest play . . . [he] has seen"[17] for some time. Similarly, Mel Gussow notes that Wilson's characters belong "to an immutable past where trains were on time and where playwrights could afford to be sentimental and unfashionable."[18] Its combination of sweet and sour sentiment with often raucous comedy contributed to its success with audiences and, on the whole, with critics, too.

Though elegiac in nature, the play is far from being a sentimental indulgence in nostalgia for a bygone age, although there is clearly a hankering after a more compassionate society. This is not, however, a view that is shared by some; Edith Oliver dismissed the work entirely on first viewing, calling it sentimental in the extreme; her opinion was not much improved by a second exposure: "I must record a negative vote," she says, "I liked it better the second time I saw it, and laughed aloud a few times, [but] I still don't believe it."[19] She went on to note how "the characters seem derived more from literature than from life. They are characterizations, not people."[20] This view is, however, distinctly at odds with that of Harold Clurman, who notes with some glee "what a relief it is to come upon a slice of *life*, rather than a contraption of showmanship or aesthetic pretension!"[21]

The Hotl Baltimore is one of Wilson's most humorous pieces and includes many pointed—and often hilarious—reminders of life's harshness. With many vinegary asides and flatly dismissive pragmatism, he punctures any superficial romanticism. The worldly prostitute April provides much of the humor of the play; she is extremely quick-witted and, in another life, could surely have been a comedienne. She is particularly adept at squashing high-flown sentiments, and her scathing put-downs and verbal deflations pervade the work. She sees through her companions' self-deluding—and usually impossible—reveries and dreams, reducing them to cruel, though amusing, reality.

Tiring of the Girl's endless quest to find Paul's grandfather, April punctures her reveries with a quip that alludes to two details of the George Washington myth: his destruction of the trees and his honesty. Says April: "Ought to be easy enough to find. Ten-foot white-haired giant. Chops down cherry trees; doesn't lie about it" (act 3, p. 66). Similarly, when the Girl muses whimsically about the future of the condemned hotel and fantasizes about possible romantic associations in its distant past, April is ready with her verbal demolition technique:

> *Girl.* I wonder what's gonna be where my room is? I mean, in that space of air? That space will still be up there where I lived. We probably walk right under and right past the places where all kinds of things happened. A tepee or a log cabin might have stood right

where I'm standing. Wonderful things might have happened right
on this spot.
April. Davy Crockett might have crapped on the stairs. Pocahontas
might of got laid by—(act 1, p. 25)

Later, a wistful reminiscence of the unspoilt joys of old America
is summarily punctured:

Girl. Baltimore used to be one of the most beautiful cities in America.
April. Every city in America used to be one of the most beautiful
cities in America. (act 3, p. 62)

Thus, in the midst of broad comedy, Wilson inserts a poignant
aside that becomes, ironically, more forceful because of its light-
hearted context. No doubt the wistfulness and nostalgia are genuine, but Wilson remains astute and skilled enough in his writing
to be able to balance the romance with prosaic reality and thereby
to enjoy the best of both worlds.

April's pragmatism is certainly not appreciated by her less re-
silient colleagues, who see her as impossibly hardened and irre-
trievably cynical. Her efforts to bring the dizzy prostitute Suzy
down to earth by sneering at her dreams of ever finding a man
who will care for her, rather than merely act as another pimp, are
met with bitter hostility:

April. All you have to say to a hooker is cottage small by the waterfall
and they fold up.
Suzy. You know I don't appreciate that word.
April. Whadda you call it?
Suzy. I am not a that-word; I am a friendly person and it gets me
in trouble.
Arpil. You're a professional trampoline. (act 3, pp. 63–64)

The humor is not, however, confined to the witticisms of prostitutes; Wilson imbues the play with throwaway comedic lines that
may serve little purpose as far as plot development is concerned,
but do shed light on the kind of people who reside, or have re-
sided, in the hotel. For example, the management decide that a
one-time tenant named Horse is not to be allowed back because
"He's crazy. He don't make sense. He don't talk sense" (act 1, p.
26). Mr. Katz explains to Horse's mother that: "Last time I let him

come back he stole the telephone outta his room. Tried to sell it back to the hotel. Said there was no telephone in his room" (ibid.). The almost senile Mr. Morse's frequent arguments and tendency to burst into song at inappropriate moments punctuate the play like a persistent exclamation mark, and Mrs. Belotti's explanations of the tragedies that have befallen both her diabetic husband and her half-witted son are almost painful in their inadvertent comedy.

The sparky, if almost exhausted, resilience of its characters ultimately make the work an uplifting, rather than a depressing, experience. Wilson has stated that, for him, the play is primarily about "losers refusing to lose,"[22] and he insists that he never once considered his characters to be anything but stalwart survivors in a hostile world:

> To me they're brave people. They are survivors, and I have always thought that this would be obvious in the writing. But some reviewers seem to miss this, and believe that the play is about a pack of dead-beats, and it isn't what I had in mind at all. . . . In this work I was trying to be both honest and positive and, despite the sadness, I think it succeeds. It *is* a comedy with some pathos; if you were to draw a graph of it, it would begin to turn up at the end just a little bit.[23]

The inhabitants of *The Hotl Baltimore* may be outside society, with futile dreams, but they refuse to be defeated. Each has aspirations and hopes, as is forcefully articulated by, ironically, the grasping, selfish Jackie when she cries in anguish: "I got dreams, goddamnit!" (act 2, p. 50). Toward the end, the Girl provides its *raison d'être:* "I don't think it matters what someone believes in. I just think it's really chicken not to believe in anything!" (act 3, p. 67).

The play's final image of April and Jamie, still unaware that he has been abandoned by his sister, dancing in the hotel's lobby combines an unutterable sadness with a feeling of hope for the future, of acceptance of what fate has to offer. In one sense, Jamie has been cast aside, but in another he is free for the first time in his life; exactly what this freedom implies is ambiguous, but Wilson suggests that the boy's future prospects may be brighter than his stifled present. At the very least, he is at last in active communication with another individual. Wilson intends the tableau to be a positive one:

The image of April and Jamie drinking champagne and dancing, round and round in circles in the middle of a hotel that is to be torn down . . . that is to do with the acceptance of life, of mortality, but not defeat.[24]

Although there may be considerable irony in the "coupling" of the worldly and cynical April with the innocent Jamie, as John Simon has noted, "Wilson understands the interplay of the absurd and the miraculous—indeed, their very identity—and how it sustains life."[25] The human comedy continues; life goes on. The Girl casts aside her disappointments and goes upstairs for a bath; a pizza is delivered; the others drift away as April and Jamie dance. As Ann Crawford Dreher observes, this pungent ending "implies that the brave sing and dance in the teeth of destruction."[26]

Each of Wilson's urban dramas utilizes metaphor to illustrate the playwright's dramatic rationale. This is nowhere more strongly demonstrated than in *The Hotl Baltimore*. Here, virtually everything is symbolic; he has stated that the work "chronicles the effects of decay; what the people have done to the city, what the city has done to them".[27]

In his stage directions, Wilson seizes an opportunity to include a pointed observation on ephemerality: "The theater, evanescent itself, and for all we do perhaps itself disappearing here, seems the ideal place for the representation of the impermanence of our architecture."[28] This is echoed by Marshall Mason who observes that "the subject of *The Hotl Baltimore* is really the hotel itself, and the way the architecture stands for the crumbling of America."[29]

Metaphor is even present in the eccentric title, which is left unexplained, but presumably denotes an unseen broken neon sign proclaiming the hotel's name. The "e" has disappeared along with the former grandeur of the establishment, leaving an incomplete and suitably tawdry reminder of the current state of the decrepit hotel.

That the Girl is left unnamed is also significant; Wilson suggests that she too is ephemeral, endlessly adaptable to any environment, willing to bend to any shape in order to survive. She is unable even to settle on a suitable name for herself; during the course of the play she goes from the prosaic and down-to-earth Martha to the excessively floral Lilac Lavender. She is aided and abetted by the other characters, who indulge her fantasy name-changing and shifts of identity. The instability of the Girl's character is also echoed in the fact that she claims to have been to "every state in the Union. Some of them three times." (act 2, p. 41).

Wilson laments the passing of his much-loved railroads, particularly in comparison to the impersonality of mass air travel. He loathes flying and will go to great lengths to avoid it. His distaste for travelling by air coheres with his attack on the contemporary trend toward pointless speed and the consequent deterioration of other forms of transport—and, by implication, of the quality of life. He has observed that:

> The condemned hotel in the play is a symbol, a symbol of the way people were welcomed at a time when this nation travelled more leisurely. I hate airplanes—we go from terminal to terminal without ever seeing the land—and I knew early in the play that there would be a long aching lament for the last railroad.[30]

In this exchange, Wilson manages humorously to combine his distaste for flying with an economical evocation of the Girl's intellectual grasp:

> *Girl.* . . . I really have no use for airplanes; I'd be just as happy if every one fell into the sea like what's his name.
> *Paul.* Icarus.
> *Girl.* No, it was Gary Cooper or Cary Grant; I get them all mixed up. (act 3, p. 60)

Like the Girl, Wilson is "a railroad freak."[31] He recalls how, as a youth, he was totally obsessed with the beauty of the old railroads; he would spend hours just watching trains passing by. While writing *The Hotl Baltimore,* he once again travelled a great deal by rail:

> I started reliving my infatuation with trains. At every station, I would go in and look at these glorious stations, not falling down, but derelict, built very well. Strong, but abandoned.[32]

Wilson's views on modern transport are summed up in the Girl's outburst, when she hears a train in the distance that should have arrived hours before:

Girl. (*Angry*) There's no schedule involved in it. I don't think they
have schedules any more. Silver Star is due in at four-nineteen;
she's more than three damn hours late. I get so mad at them for
not running on time. I mean it's their own damn schedule, I don't
know why they can't keep to it. They're just miserable. The service
is so bad and hateful, and the porters and conductors, you just can't
believe it isn't deliberate. I think they're being run by the airlines.
(act 1, p. 14)

The late arrival of the Silver Star thus becomes a powerful symbol
for the slackening of all good practice and high standards, since
it underscores the apparent lack of care exhibited by the authori-
ties. The main source of the Girl's disappointment in the play,
Paul Granger III, is similarly linked to her by the fact that his
grandfather was an engineer for the Baltimore and Ohio railroad,
(act 2, p. 48). This only increases her desire to help Paul find him,
despite Paul's assertions that he does not need her assistance;
indeed, he resents her interference. However, she persists until,
finally, he rejects her and she is devastated.

The Girl acts as a metaphor for steadfastness and constancy;
she retains faith in the basic goodness of those she meets and is
always willing to help in any way she can. "I want everything. . . .
For everybody. . . . I want everyone to have everything," she says
(act 1, p. 29). Not for a moment does she permit herself to despair,
believing, perhaps naively, that happiness is just around the
corner.

For this character, almost every memory is a rosy one; everything in the past was perfect. She recalls how, when she was a
child, "it used to rain and then it'd be sunny . . . immediately"
(ibid.), and she quickly follows this with "It almost never rained
anyway. But when it did, just the next day all the cactus would
bloom all over" (ibid.). For the Girl, admitting rain to have fallen
at all in the golden days of her youth must be quickly countered by
a positive image of regeneration. As Michiko Kakutani observes,
however, "in using memory to romanticize the past . . . [Wilson's]
characters perpetuate their illusions—the same way they so skil-
fully use verbal pyrotechnics to conceal their vulnerabilities."[33]

That the Girl is frequently met with apathy or even hostility is
Wilson's way of dramatizing the difficulties of establishing friend-

ship and trust; good intentions are frequently spurned or miscon-
strued due to mistrust of the motives involved or a wish to remain
uncommitted. Because of her sunny personality and unshakable
optimism, such rebuffs will, it is suggested, leave little impact upon
the Girl's favorable estimate of humanity's fundamental decency.

Like *Balm in Gilead*, this work is filled with music, both metaphorically, in the sense of its characters moving in rhythmic se-
quences as they enter and exit the stage, and in the literal music
emanating from the radio on the front desk. Of the latter Wilson,
in his introductory notes, directs:

> . . . the play is designed to incorporate music popular during produc-
> tion. The music plays in the theater before the acts, and as the lights
> dim, the sound fades into the radio on stage. At the end of the acts
> the radio music builds again, moving into the house. The first and
> third acts should end with a positive song with an upbeat, a song that
> one has heard in passing a dozen times but never listened to closely.[34]

In his original staging, Marshall Mason made much of this. He
describes how he infused the concluding moments of the second
act with a musical motif that both informed and elaborated upon
the action:

> We used a lot of contemporary music to bridge the intermissions in
> my production so that, for example, at the end of the second act,
> when Jackie has stolen Mr. Morse's sock and they have their great
> contretemps ending with her cry from the heart "I got dreams god-
> damnit, what's he got?," a stunned silence follows. Jackie leaves, every-
> thing is a mess, and Mr. Morse goes sadly upstairs. Meanwhile, the
> hotel staff changes and Bill arrives to start the new day; he turns on
> the radio and, just as it is beginning to play, Millie—on her way up-
> stairs, too—turns and suddenly says "Your grandfather is alive, Paul,"
> and he says "How do you know?" and she says, "I never know how I
> know, I just know." And, immediately, we hear from the radio, The
> Moody Blues with "I'm looking for someone to change my life, I'm
> looking for a miracle in my life." And the whole thing comes together;
> it's as though Lanford wrote the song, it fitted in so perfectly.[35]

Wilson extends the musical analogy by describing some of his
characters according to their lyrical propensities: for example,
Mr. Katz and Bill Lewis are baritones; Paul Granger III is a tenor;
Millie has "a lovely voice"; Suzy is definitely a mezzo.[36]

The Hotl Baltimore is a play suffused with the concept of ephemerality, of time passing and changing, and of the necessity to hold on to the firm realities of days gone by. It also acknowledges that the effort is all; to strive and dream are the essential factors, even if the ultimate result is out of our control. In this play, Wilson considers issues similar to those explored in T. S. Eliot's "East Coker," in *The Four Quartets,* whose words seem to express the playwright's vision:

> There is only the fight to recover what has been lost
> And found and lost again and again: and now, under conditions
> That seem unpropitious. But perhaps neither gain nor loss.
> For us, there is only the trying. The rest is not our business.[37]

The inhabitants of *The Hotl Baltimore* will, despite their resistance, be forced to move on, but they take with them their aspirations and a sense of what has made them what they are; their memories are precious and worth preserving. Wilson's dramatic feelings seem crystallized in the words of the eccentric, though essentially wise, Millie, who believes that the ghosts who inhabit the Hotel will "stay around for a while wondering what's become of everything. Then they'll wander off with people . . . [and] form attachments" (act 1, p. 1). Change is inevitable and must be confronted, if not overcome. But scraps of life remain among the dust of memory; old times may fade, but their recollection is a source of constant renewal.

5

Burn This

My passions have made me live and my passions have killed me
—Rousseau

Burn This is an extraordinarily rich and complex work that both encompasses and expands upon almost every dramatic idea ever expressed by Wilson—while adding a few more. It is, effectively, the cumulative representation of all of his interests and obsessions. Here he explores sexual fascination and love, loss and grief, the formation of nontraditional familial groups, fear of urban life, homosexuality, the forced trendiness of modern New York living and its associated decline in oral communication, frustration, artistic creativity, loneliness, violence, and broad comedy. A rich texture is afforded by themes that at first appear diverse and unconnected, but soon meld to form a complex and satisfying drama.

Permeating the work is the leitmotif of loss, the impact of an artist's untimely death. For Wilson, the play was a personal challenge and even a kind of catharsis in that he wrote it following the death of a close friend, an artist who lived in Sag Harbor, New York, where the playwright resides. Wilson has stated that the somewhat cryptic title relates to an admonition a writer might add to the head of each page of a particularly personal letter or essay. If the author constantly reminds himself that what is being written is so private that it can be burned if necessary, without being seen by anyone else, he might be encouraged to release his inhibitions and commit the absolute truth to paper. Thus, when Wilson began work on this play in the fall of 1985, he wrote the words "burn this" at the top of every page, to spur himself to be as open and as honest as possible. No vulnerability was to be spared, no pain unconfronted. Ironically, it is Burton, the high-flying but rather shallow screenwriter in the play, who actually describes the title: "Make it as personal as you can . . . Make it personal, tell the truth, and then write 'Burn this' on it" (act 2, p. 60).

Robert Allan Ackerman, director of the London productions of the play, describes the creative process involved:

> . . . after you have expressed your most personal thoughts, especially as a writer or any artist, once you've expressed your most personal, most naked self, you have the option then to destroy it, but the important thing is to go through the process of expressing and searching and looking inside yourself for those very, very personal thoughts, the artistic expression of them. It is the process that is important.[1]

In many ways, *Burn This* is a song of innocence and experience. During the years leading up to Robbie's death and her meeting with Pale, Anna has largely avoided confronting genuine emotion and has maintained an almost adolescent innocence. Her apparent dedication to dance has, in reality, had little more depth than the strangulated screenplays of her lover, Burton, which always strive toward important and epic themes, but remain resolutely earthbound and faintly ludicrous. Experiences were not something in which this couple became involved, but merely events that occurred without really touching them.

Anna does seem to have genuine creative potential where Burton does not, but, as Lou Liberatore (who has played Larry since the play's inception) observes, she has compromised her talents in the name of leading a "beautiful but shallow existence, making cute little dances that look pretty but really go nowhere."[2] To create, one must first experience, and Anna's experience evolves out of the rigorous emotional shaking she receives from Pale. Marshall Mason believes Pale represents

> all that is uncivilized; what we don't like to deal with in life; these are perhaps the sources that the artist must draw from: the deep fears, the awful guilts, the horrors.[3]

Wilson confirms this, observing that

The play has to do with art and what you have to know and what you
have to go through before you can do anything worthwhile; before
you are able to produce something that people will recognize and
believe in. Pale allows Anna to become an artist; he makes her live
again.[4]

At least one critic has suggested that the apparently philistine
Pale is the only true artist in the play, calling it "a play about art
in which the strongest sensibility belongs to a character who looks
upon artists as frauds."[5] Certainly Pale believes in his own creative
potential, stating that he "could've been a dancer" (act 1, p. 39)
and that he has composed "whole symphonies . . . tone poems,
concertos . . . huge big orchestrations" (ibid.) in the shower. Just
how seriously we are meant to take this is unclear, although John
Malkovich (Pale in both American and British productions of the
work) believes that he *may* have artistic abilities that have been
ground down over the years: "He sees himself as a creative person,
but he's never had the chance to do anything about it. That's one
reason why he resents his brother's success as an artist."[6]

Although Pale may have an artistic temperament, he cannot
really be regarded as an artist because he does not create art—
although he certainly facilitates its expression in Anna. His reaction to the world may be vibrant and sensitive, but that does not
make him an artist, despite what he says. *Burn This* stresses the
necessity of committing oneself, of taking responsibility. It is insufficient, Wilson seems to be saying, merely to have unfulfilled ideas
in one's head without committing them to paper or acting them
out; it is essential to write it down, to express it, to create something of importance. After this, if necessary, it can be destroyed.

A clear progression can be traced from *Balm in Gilead* to *Burn
This*. In some respects the two works could hardly be more different—the social milieus are completely dissimilar—but there are
in fact many similarities. The sheer energy that permeates *Burn
This*, its characters' intensity of expression, and its raw emotion
coupled with the bleakest comedy clearly link it with the earlier
play. Similarly, the language Wilson uses here is closer to *Balm in
Gilead* than to any other play. For example, Pale's "tree speech"
(act 1, p. 35) is written in a stream of consciousness style similar
to that of Dopey's cockroach monologue (act 1, pp. 26–27). Wilson

describes the surrealism of such language as having "a logic that is very special, very tenuous, and very specific to that character's train of thought."[7]

Many of the plays Wilson wrote between the two appear to move away consciously from the rawness of expression common to both toward a milder, more overtly poetic kind of drama. In works such as *The Hot l Baltimore*, for example, Wilson continued to mold what appears to be ordinary speech into poetry, but his method had become far more subtle; the lyricism had no separate existence and blended invisibly into the whole. During the years that followed, Wilson continued to work in this vein, his refinement of language becoming more and more extreme, perhaps climaxing in *Angels Fall*, written in 1983. This play is virtually a tone poem, so finely attenuated, so filled with what Marshall Mason calls "soft and gentle grace notes,"[8] its language and action so subtly and completely integrated that it could scarcely become more genteel without risking blandness.

Wilson became aware of this continuing tendency in his writing when he saw a revival of *Balm in Gilead*, and immediately set about writing *Burn This* with the intention from the outset to consciously link the two works in an effort to recapture some of the creative energy he felt he had lost:

> I had just seen John Malkovich's revival of *Balm in Gilead* and I thought, God, I used to have such incredible energy; where has all that energy and imagination gone? . . . so in *Burn This* I was trying to get back some of that energy and put it into the kind of plays I write now. Also, I think some of the play could be interpreted as Pale being representative of *Balm in Gilead* and the other three characters standing for myself, just so complacent and sophisticated and above it all . . . so Pale is there to goose the others— and myself—into doing something fresh and worthwhile.[9]

Malkovich clearly agrees with this assessment, seeing the work as Wilson's

> attempt to get back to a kind of raw—rawer—perhaps darker—expression . . . away from the Talley plays. Some of Lanford's earlier plays like *Balm in Gilead, Home Free!* and *The Madness of Lady Bright* are unbelievably dark. *Burn This* is similar.[10]

This is further borne out by Marshall Mason who notes that:

> There's a kind of harkening back to Lanford's earlier impulses here; he wanted to move away from being overtly poetic and refined and to find again the danger and energy of his early work, although there is still much to admire in the poetry of *Burn This*. Pale breaks into the beautiful, rather artificial world that Lanford has created and explodes it . . . . Pale's energy comes from the same place as that in *Balm in Gilead*; in fact, the two works are very similar in many ways.[11]

The extent of Mason's contributions to and involvement in the development of Wilson's work has changed over the years. In some works his involvement has been considerable; on occasion, he "insisted certain things had to be changed and served almost as an in-house critic."[12] To *Burn This*, however, his contribution was minimal:

> I really haven't had a lot to do with it. In this play Lanford has looked for those forces in our urban life that are huge and undeniable and that we spend a lot of our civilized life avoiding. We think of civilization as protecting us from the abyss, but in fact our civilization has itself become a force to be reckoned with.[13]

The play hinges on the sudden death of Robbie, an unseen gay man who has died in a boating accident while out with his boyfriend. Although Robbie never appears, he is crucial to the work; the crisis and change that his death precipitates in each of the onstage characters forces them to confront their inadequacy and vulnerability, as well as their fears of mortality. His importance was deeply felt by Robert Allan Ackerman; during rehearsals, the cast would improvise situations that might occur had Robbie actually been in the work.

> We spent a lot of time talking about Robbie, and what the others would have done if he had actually been there, and what he meant and represented to each of them. We all felt that he was as important a character as anyone on the stage, so fundamental was his impact on their lives.[14]

Robbie's ability to influence the lives of his friends extends even beyond death; as a result of the accident, they are introduced to his elder brother. In the early hours of the morning, Jimmy (known as Pale, because of his fondness for VSOP brandy), erupts into the play with volcanic rage, ostensibly to collect his brother's belongings. Nothing is ever the same again. Pale brings with him the dangers, the gross realities, and the seamier aspects of New York street life. However, his invasion also brings with it vibrancy and passion, raw truth, and, for Anna, the possibility of genuine and unfettered love.

A major concern in *Burn This* is undoubtedly love—not a love that is in any way clichéd or romanticized, but one that engulfs and transforms. Wilson has stated that he set out to write an adult love story, but one that tackled and elucidated issues usually ignored or side-stepped by most authors. He recalls:

> I was trying to push myself further than I had gone in a love story. I had seen thousands of love stories and I always felt they didn't go far enough; they didn't show what really happens . . . I wanted to write about what love really is and how sexual it is and how *beyond* sexual it is, how it transforms and the sacrifices that you have to make, what you have to go through to find someone to love.[15]

Similarly, Tanya Berezin observes that

> *Burn This* deals with love itself; not really romantic love—although the play is astonishingly sexual—but real love. It is a question of giving up part of yourself in order to let another person into your life.[16]

Throughout *Burn This*, Wilson stresses the need for emotional involvement and risk-taking, even when this may seem foolhardy or, indeed, dangerous. In the relationship that develops between Pale and Anna, the play finds its *raison d'être*: a plea for commitment to a loving relationship despite the potential hazards inherent in sexual contact. Better to experience the pain of a genuine loving relationship, Wilson seems to urge, than merely to exist in bland mediocrity.

He cites Iris Murdoch's novel *A Severed Head* as having made a contribution to the play. In this work, the protagonists embark upon a potentially destructive, certainly enervating, love affair that Wilson describes as "a collision course relationship. The man asks the woman if they will ever be happy, and she replies 'Happy has nothing to do with this.' Their relationship just has to *be*."[17]

Burn This has proven to be one of Wilson's most successful ventures, both critically and at the box office. An important focus for the attention it received by the media was undoubtedly ex-Steppenwolf actor John Malkovich's extraordinarily feral, yet sensitive, central performance as Pale. This was hailed, almost without exception, as a landmark in contemporary acting. His interpretation of Pale is so central to the play that it bears close scrutiny here; Wilson had written half of the role before he saw Malkovich in action and then completed it with him in mind. It is difficult to conceive of the play *without* the strength of Malkovich's portrayal, so perfectly does he adapt the demands of the work to his powerful acting technique.

Malkovich was one of the founding members of the Steppenwolf Theatre Company, based in Highland Park, Chicago. Between its inception in 1976 and 1982, Malkovich acted in, directed, or designed sets for over fifty productions. The Company is noted for the passion, creativity, and energy of its performers, and for their original—often unsettling—productions of contemporary and classic plays. Malkovich is, to date, the most famous Steppenwolf alumnus working both in the theatre and in such films as *The Killing Fields, Death of a Salesman, Dangerous Liaisons, The Sheltering Sky, The Object of Beauty,* and *Of Mice and Men,* but many of the original members have made successful careers in theatre and film.

During a BBC programme dedicated to the work of Malkovich, Laurie Metcalf, a long-time member of the Company, theorized about how the dynamic and often overtly aggressive techniques adopted by the Company have evolved and noted that they have been variously described as "rock and roll" or risk-taking;[18] John Mahoney, another Steppenwolf member, described the Company's approach as profoundly intense, whether acting Noël Coward or Sam Shepard; the sheer *intensity* of application that the Company brings to each of the works it performs is its most notable trait.[19]

The Steppenwolf method of acting certainly found a willing and creative interpreter in Malkovich whose primary aim as an actor is to present in as honest and direct a manner as possible salient aspects of the human condition. If this involves aggression or violence, so be it; he seizes upon such opportunities to depict the truth of those he portrays. He acknowledges that he does, perhaps, have more anger and aggression in his personality than most people,[20] but insists that this is channelled and focused during performance. Michael Billington believes that Malkovich has "great presence"[21] and believes that:

> ... what Malkovich brings onstage in *Burn This* is first of all a sense of danger, unpredictability, wildness ... you never quite know with Malkovich what he is going to do next. And I think danger is crucial to good acting .... that quality that you find in nearly all the best American acting—the ability to live the moment; it's an extraordinary ability, to concentrate that .. intensity onstage.[22]

Milton Shulman described Malkovich's interpretation of Pale as "rampaging, threatening, mesmeric,"[23] while Jack Tinker commented upon his "wall-blasting intensity."[24]

Aggression and ferocity were not, however, the only aspects of his performance that attracted attention. There is a peculiar kind of virile effeminacy about Pale that Malkovich shares and that he explored to the full in creating the role. Robert Allan Ackerman recalls Malkovich's feminine characteristics as constituting

> a particularly telling part of his nature. In the tea-making scene when he cossets that kettle and makes what must be the best cup of tea in the world, he presents such a wonderful image; in that woman's bathrobe with his long hair, cleaning up like some Italian housewife.[25]

Similarly, Michael Simkins believes that, without this aspect of Malkovich's performance, the play could easily have fallen into a typically heterosexual/homosexual comedy of manners:

> There is a very feminine air to Malkovich. Feminine but not effeminate. By openly exploring that part of his personality, he gave the production colossal strength .... That was one of the wonders: his being able to be both toweringly powerful and delicately vulnerable, almost at the same moment. Instead of the gay element becoming compartmentalized, John's performance allowed something of that to run through the play. It marbled the whole work. I am sure there were audiences who thought that Larry and Pale would end up together![26]

Pale's persona is in some ways very close to that projected by Malkovich himself, and it is interesting to note Bernardo Bertolucci's opinion of the actor. After directing him in the film version of Paul Bowles's *The Sheltering Sky*, where he plays the complex central character—an emotionally deracinated musician abroad in a desert landscape—Bertolucci saw him in *Burn This*. To him, the actor represented the perfect manifestation of the existential hero: attractive though lonely, hardened by life's experience yet vulnerable, tough but at the same time curiously delicate.[27] Thus, violence and sweetness of nature coexist; a seemingly impermeable surface is, in reality, as fragile as glass.

The potency and complexity of Malkovich's acting have led a number of critics to compare him to the young Marlon Brando. For example, Kenneth Hurren cited Brando's performance as Stanley Kowalski in Williams' *A Streetcar Named Desire* as an apt forerunner.[28] Irving Wardle wrote that Malkovich brought to the play "the animal magnetism of Brando's Stanley Kowalski,"[29] and Michael Billington felt that, "like Brando [Malkovich] combines an imploding intensity with sudden, revealing touches of feminine gentleness."[30] For his performance in the London productions of *Burn This*, Malkovich was nominated for various theatre awards and won the Time Out Awards Best Actor prize for 1990.

Although it is never made explicit, *Burn This* is also an exploration of the effects of AIDS on those its victims leave behind. Wilson has stated that Robbie's character is symbolic of the AIDS virus, in that his untimely and tragic demise is perhaps occasioned by the fact that he is homosexual. Much ambiguity surrounds his death; there is an underlying suggestion in the play that, because of Robbie's openness about his homosexuality—he even broadcast it on national television—he has been murdered by sinister and hostile forces within his own family or by the Mafia. Pale certainly regards Robbie's death as "No fuckin' accident," (act 2, p. 70) and tells Anna that "the mob did it" (ibid.). Later, Anna relates another of Pale's anecdotes to Larry:

> *Anna.* . . . [Pale] was saying he and his dad and their cronies got to drinking, someone says I saw your fruit brother on the TV with his boyfriend. All the usual fag-baiting braggadocio. Someone ought to off the fucker, embarrassment to the family, that crap. And a couple of nights later, Robbie's dead. (act 2, pp. 74, 75)

Tanya Berezin elaborates on this possibility:

Robbie dies, and on one level there is the question of whether he dies because he is gay, and I think that is the connection with AIDS in a concrete, though symbolic, way. Does Robbie's family have Mafia connections who want him out of the way? It's possible, but we simply do not know. The untimely loss of what is assumed to be a major talent is something that we in the theatre and the arts have been going through for the last ten years, and this is Lanford's way of dramatizing such loss.[31]

Similarly, Marshall Mason observes that:

Although AIDS is referred to only very indirectly, the play is saturated with its consequences. The resultant intense feelings of loss and frustration—here epitomized by Pale—are only too familiar to those in the arts who have lost friends and colleagues.[32]

The specter of AIDS moves insidiously through the lives of all the characters, forcing them to adapt their sexual habits and to protect themselves in any way they can. Perhaps the most tragic figure in the play is Larry, despite his wisecracking persona and ironic acceptance of his lot. He is alone, without a partner, living vicariously through the relationships of those around him.

After Burton's recollection of his homosexual experience in the snow, Larry wistfully observes, "Lord, the innocence and freedom of yesterday" (act 2, p. 63). Full of camp bravado, Larry is nonetheless clearly terrified; he rejects the possibility of a serious relationship because of his fears, and he does not even manage to attend the gay New Year's Eve party where, he says, "the suicide rate is higher than all of Scandinavia combined" (act 2, p. 57).

Robert Allan Ackerman describes Larry's life as being "in a very sorry state . . . because of AIDS, he is living in a city where gay life has completely had the lid put on, and where everyone is very, very afraid."[33] Larry is thus imprisoned because of his fear of contracting the disease; when even the formation of a loving, sexual relationship can result in a fatal illness, a carefully cultivated survival strategy must be developed; in Larry's case, this takes the form of completely opting out of a sexual life. Lou Liberatore notes that

Larry doesn't really know how sad he is until the end of the play; it really hits him then and he asks what he has done with his life. He has to face something very, very painful.[34]

Larry's marginalization enables Wilson to utilize him as a kind of mordantly witty chorus whose remarks both contribute to and comment on the action around him. He acts as a filter for the rest of the proceedings, the constant that allows the variables of the play to interact in a far more candid fashion than if he did not exist, facilitating the emotional interaction of others. Tragically, his fear of involvement precludes his own participation in similar scenarios. As Liberatore says,

Larry is the lynch-pin. A lot hinges on him. Because he is the outsider in a way, and not really part of the relationships onstage, he can balance the other characters, keep things in order, stop them from getting out of hand. He is the objective chorus that allows the audience to understand and participate in the work. It would be too frightening to watch the violent scene between Pale and Anna without Larry's presence; he deflects the tension and keeps it tolerable. He is far more than mere wisecracks and gay humor.[35]

Although Larry's predicament is perhaps the saddest in the play, AIDS stains the lives of its heterosexual characters, too. Juliet Stevenson, who played Anna in the London productions of the play, identifies the terrible irony of a fatal virus that attacks the very core of human relationships:

AIDS is so horrible, so evil, because even if you sleep with somebody, one of the most natural and normal human things you can do and, ironically, what should bring people together, you are endangering yourself and the other person. You become contaminated.[36]

In such a climate, intimate relationships *can* flourish, but they are often superficial and unfulfilling. For the most part, safe mediocrity is preferable to unpredictable passion. Until she meets Pale, and a different, vibrant world opens up for her, Anna has, in the main, sought solace and affection from her male homosexual friends—indeed, she has shared her apartment with two of them for a number of years. By comparison, her relationship with Burton appears to be rather sterile, a compromise, although the love on his part seems genuine enough.

The concept of AIDS, thus infecting the play and forming an apt and very modern metaphor for fear of human involvement, permits Wilson to explore the complexities of sexual mores in contemporary New York. However, Wilson utilizes its metaphorical potency in more than one way. While it permits him to illustrate emotional compromise in three of his characters, it also allows him to exemplify the antithesis in the character of Pale.

Here is a man who may have yielded to pressure and compromise in the past, but who has now reached breaking point. His brother's death and his own sense of guilt, frustration, and remorse have combined to sharpen his pain. Realizing that he has failed his brother by rejecting him because of homosexuality, Pale has also always resented Robbie's success as a dancer—an artist who could enjoy freedom of expression through his work. Furthermore, Pale has ruined any chance of happiness with his own wife and family and has betrayed himself and his own potential; he can no longer cope with this overwhelming frustration save by excessive drinking and drug abuse. Carrying so much pain within him, he is exhausted from the effort of living.

Pale feels *everything* keenly. As if his intense guilt and the acknowledgment of his own failure were not enough, he also recognizes that the life he has lived till now has been a sham and that most of what he has believed in has also been a lie. Wilson remarks

> Pale has been done in. He has done himself in; his whole life is just a mockery of anything that he could really buy into . . . . he is, by far, one of the best examples of the walking wounded I have ever written.[37]

John Malkovich describes Pale's life experience as

> just terrible . . . he has been working his ass off his whole life. Such ridiculously hard work. He has been married since he was eighteen, just a kid, and now, at work, there's always some problem, some person who's doing something wrong, something always going wrong. He has to deal with everything, and it's killing him. He is called upon to take responsibility *constantly.*[38]

Pale represents all that is hazardous and threatening, but at the same time demonstrates an authentic, if warped, innocence and need. Full of paradoxes, he is foul-mouthed, almost insanely aggressive, and yet strangely vulnerable. For Marshall Mason, he is the embodiment of everything brutal and uncultivated,

> He is a monster of need. He typifies the basic animalistic sexual persona, the childlike take–what–you–need–when–you–need–it mentality, and the need to grab life and squeeze it. There's a primitive aspect to Pale that is very heartfelt and gutfelt, and in complete contrast to the other characters in the work who are so refined. He really shakes them up! Anna's life is so genteel, so far away from genuine feelings, of deep fears and real love. Pale awakens all this in her again.[39]

In the way that he suddenly bursts onto the scene, spitting with anger and frustration and permeating the atmosphere with his unrestrained sexuality, Pale invades the lives of the other characters as powerfully as their fear of the lethal virus. He is, however, by no means a negative character; he is the fulcrum of change on which all is finally—perhaps positively—resolved. He "gives Anna back her life"[40] and enables her to become a creative artist.

The dance that Anna eventually creates arises from the anguish of her relationship with Pale, which despite the pain, has invigorated her and facilitated an artistically truthful representation of their love affair. In creating the work, Anna undergoes a profound catharsis and is finally liberated. Larry attempts to describe her achievement for Burton:

> *Larry.* . . . I *can* testify that the work she's doing is phenomenal . . . it's a regular man—dancing like a man dances—in a bar or something, with his girl. You've never seen anything like it. (act 2, pp. 91, 93)

Even Pale is impressed, if embarrassed, at the nakedness of the representation: "That was me and you up there. Only we ain't never danced. I could probably sue you for that" (act 2, p. 97).

Pale represents for Anna the second tidal wave of emotion that has recently engulfed her, the first being the shock of Robbie's death and her subsequent sense of loss and outrage. Because of this initial emotional upheaval she is, in a way, prepared for Pale when he bursts into her life; he matches the depth of her anger and she sees in him a kindred spirit. During rehearsals, Robert

Allan Ackerman was inspired by a Laura Nyro song entitled
"*Stony End.*" The lyrics of this always made him think of Anna:

> This song was written long before I knew the play, but it seems to be
> so pertinent. It talks about the fury and raging thunders that come
> to match a raging soul, and I believe that is what happens here with
> Anna and Pale.[41]

This is confirmed by Juliet Stevenson:

> Anna comes to recognize and accept her anger and outrage. She
> finishes the first part of act 1 in a mood of great frustration and
> resentment, recalling Robbie's funeral; she didn't have a moment
> alone to say goodbye to him and vows never to forgive his family for
> the way they treated him—and her. The next minute, anger in the
> form of Pale comes in through the door, and it's a recognition! It is
> "I"! . . . When you are in a state of extremis, and you feel your skin
> has been ripped off, everything that used to interest you or involve
> you no longer does; what Anna had now means little; everything
> needs re-evaluating. She needs Pale as the focus of her anger and
> hatred. What she feels, he feels. It is a great relief.[42]

Before the advent of Pale, Anna had relied on her relationships
with Burton, Larry, and, especially, Robbie. As the play progresses,
it gradually becomes apparent that she has long been in love with
Robbie without being able to admit or express it; suddenly, Pale
enters her life—virtually Robbie's physical double, the heterosexual embodiment of a man she has loved for years without ever
being able to satisfy her sexual frustration. She can finally realize
her dream of a love affair with the living image of an idealized
partner.

However, before Pale's arrival, Anna has endured the endless
futility of yearning for the reciprocal—physical—love of a gay
man. No doubt, her dilemma was exacerbated by the fact that she
and Robbie were both dancers and, consequently, in constant
close, physical contact with each other. As Juliet Stevenson observes,

> I believe Anna was tremendously attracted to Robbie in a very physical
> way, and that their proximity during dances and rehearsals just in-
> creased her desire for him. Their relationship stopped just short of
> them actually being lovers.[43]

Similarly, Robert Allan Ackerman describes the frustration Anna must have felt because of her sexual attraction to a gay man: "Dancers are extraordinarily physical with one another; they have their hands in each other's crotches, their legs are wrapped around each other—they are forever in intimate poses."[44]

Notwithstanding these frustrations, there is still much to be gained from platonic relationships: although painful, they can be a source of much happiness and emotional support, offering unconditional affection and loyalty. For these very reasons, however, they present their own problems. As Juliet Stevenson remarks,

> Women's relationships with gay men are so complex. I have them in my own life . . . I often find that they are most intimate and of great importance . . . . they are a source of enormous gain but also enormous loss, because you get to a point where you are safe with them and that's why they are valuable, and it's also why they are a problem to you because you can't go beyond.[45]

It was, perhaps, for this very reason that Anna's artistic relationships with Robbie could never have been very strong, despite their obvious compatibility. Indeed, such compatibility was perhaps why their work was unable to progress beyond mediocrity; it precluded any real intensity. This is borne out in comments Anna makes concerning her work and the extent of outside influences; she frets that her choreography has been shaped too much by her colleague, Charley: "I could walk down the street, it's Charley walking down the street, it isn't me" (act 1, p. 20).

In counterpoint to the inevitable compromises entailed by straight/gay friendships, Wilson comments with deadly irony—and great humor—on some of the pitfalls of heterosexual affairs. Pale and Burton are, after all, rivals for Anna's love and their physical demonstration of their affection for her is both excessive and humiliating for all concerned. They actually engage in combat over her, and endeavor to outdo each other in manly braggadocio—what Anna calls "macho bullshit" (act 2, p. 73)—circling like animals about to strike.

The result is unintentionally hysterical, as Burton constantly moves around Pale, referring to him as "fella" and "buddy" (act 2, pp. 71, 72). Since Burton is by profession a screenwriter, it is tempting to link his language here with the heroes he creates on film; certainly, his choice of words is evocative of the likes of Bruce Willis or Clint Eastwood. As if this were not embarrassing enough, Burton demonstrates his knowledge of the martial arts, while Pale laughs at his efforts, refusing to be drawn into what he considers to be a ludicrous display: "Nobody does that shit, nobody pulls that shit" (act 2, p. 71). Later, Pale calls him "Bruce" in a reference to kung fu star, Bruce Lee (act 2, p. 80). For Pale, in violent struggle as in all things, the straightforward approach is the one to adopt, his strategy is to lunge and punch, kick and trip. He pays little heed either to the etiquette of the martial arts or to the Queensborough Rules.

In an effort both to support Anna against her warring lovers and to inject some light relief into the situation, Larry eventually tries to evict Pale from her apartment by saying: "Pale? It's not as butch as Burton, but if you don't leave, I'll hit you over the head with a skillet. I'm not joking" (act 2, p. 73). At the end of this fiasco and in acknowledgment of Larry's injection of some wit and sanity, it is hardly surprising that Anna should observe that "I could live my life very well, thank you, without ever seeing another straight man" (act 2, p. 74).

Although the relationship between Anna and Burton is built on compromise (the opening lines of the play exemplify Anna's apathy: "Uh, Burton, could we make it another . . . *Sighs, buzzes him in* . . .)" (act 1, p. 6), it is by no means totally unsatisfactory. There is genuine affection on both sides, even to the extent of Anna's seriously considering getting married. Certainly Larry would be in favor of that: "I don't know why you don't just marry him and buy things" (act 1, p. 19). John Malkovich believes that Burton is "a great guy"[46] and that "the relationship between he and Anna is as strong as most."[47] In his opinion,

> Burton's just fine, but that's not necessarily enough or even what Anna wants. Therein lies the lesson. Why do women like Rhett Butler? It's because he says "I don't give a damn"; it's attractive to women. Pale has that kind of attraction for her. There's nothing wrong with Burton, though, he just isn't enough for her at that time.[48]

Burton realizes that he cannot compete with Pale, who is an unknown, alien entity, completely outside of Burton's experience and hence impossible to compete with. Burton is completely mystified that an uncouth, foul-mouthed and lower-class (certainly less wealthy) man has been able to steal Anna from him. Clearly, whatever it is that Anna sees in Pale, Burton does not possess. Finally, however, he realizes that he has never really deserved Anna. Michael Simkins notes:

> He is basically a good guy, but so full of himself. All those forced anecdotes! What saves him is that he finally realizes in the last scene with Larry that he just isn't good enough; it has all been slightly phony, slightly unreal. He *is* a poseur, but a poseur with redeeming qualities. He's not a bad fellow. Anna could have done a lot worse.[49]

In his setting of the work, Wilson extends the metaphor of restraint that, before Pale's invasion, has epitomized the characters' lives. The action takes place in a converted New York loft in the artistic environs of Lower Manhattan, the minimalist decor and nonchalant sophistication being described as "the sort of place that you would kill for or wouldn't be caught dead in" (p. 5). Pale certainly remains deeply unimpressed with the loft, constantly complaining about the heat, describing it as "a empty fuckin' warehouse" (act 1, p. 32), and deriding its supposedly desirable location overlooking the river:

> Pale. (*Looking out the window*) That's the bay, huh, the river? Jesus. What a thing to look at. Oh, look, darling, they got tugboats pushin', like, these flatcars; like, five flatcars piled about a mile high with all this city garbage and shit. Who the fuck wants to look at that? You pay for a view of that? Maybe there's people find that fascinating, that's not what I call a view. (act 1, p. 30)

Pale cannot comprehend the attraction of such a view or of living in close proximity to the city's rubbish; he despises what he sees as a middle-class affectation, a desire to be close to "reality" without actually confronting it. As a working-class man for whom such realities are only too common, this ersatz realism is a ready target.

The loft's stark, simplistic design—no frills or obvious signs of conspicuous wealth—offers a specious sense of security to its tenants; once locked behind their reinforced steel doors, they pretend that nothing can harm them, and they persuade themselves that they are safe, in control of their lives, and able to survive.

John Malkovich identifies the fundamental difference between Pale's attitude to the terrors of New York and that of the cosseted loft-dwellers:

> These characters in their expensive apartment are, metaphorically, like people who don't know, or don't want to know, that there is a maniac killer in it, whereas Pale knows full well that the danger always exists, and that the killer is there all the time.[50]

Their security is thus essentially illusory; though reluctant to admit it, because any acknowledgment may somehow make it a reality, Wilson's tenants conduct their lives behind a veil of barely suppressed panic masquerading as sophisticated irony.

The relationship that develops between Pale and Anna enables her not only to flourish as an artist, but to cope better with the pressures of city living. His practicality and strength rub off on her and transform long-pent-up terrors into endurable burdens. Born of a wealthy family in suburban Highland Park (which Lou Liberatore describes as "very nice, rich suburbs, very Kennedy"[51]) Anna has led a very sheltered life; watched over by both Robbie and Burton, she has never had to fend for herself or accept real criticism.

In truth, she has seldom had to take responsibility for anything important. As Larry observes, "She's had a very protected life. I mean, she's never had to even carry her own passport or plane tickets—she's not had to make her own way much." (act 2, p. 94). Moreover, life in New York has gradually eroded what stamina and resilience she originally possessed; paranoia about the dangers of the city has caused her to lead a careful unadventurous life, marked by caution, superficiality, and undue circumspection. Suddenly exposed to grief and raw fear, she naturally gravitates toward a man who can offer her strength—if not stability. Juliet Stevenson analyzes it thus:

> You can understand the attraction of that kind of animal strength, because at least if someone like Pale was on your side it would be a bonus. Jeanette Winterson's *Sexing the Cherry* is so entitled because it is about grafting one thing onto another and making it stronger. It's a horticultural metaphor; experts do this with cherries or apples or whatever. In a way, I think Anna grafts herself to Pale to allow herself to flourish and survive.[52]

Wilson includes much symbolism in this play: virtually every cinematic or literary allusion has a connection with the unfolding tale; even the "love story" that Burton sets out to write is probably *Burn This*. By far the most striking symbol throughout the play is heat and flame, the intensity of Pale's body temperature, the color red, passion, and, of course, the title.

Time and again, Wilson works in such references, sometimes several per page. For example, Pale sarcastically decries Anna's impatience to call the Salvation Army to pick up Robbie's clothes: "What's this huge rush? They're on fire or something? Spontaneous combustion, something?" Moments later, he hears a noise from the radiator and complains that "The fuckin' room's a oven, bake pizza here, they turn on some heat." When Anna protests that it is the middle of winter, Pale tells her: "I got like a toaster oven I carry around with me in my belly someplace. I don't use heat. I sleep the windows open, no covers" (act 1, p. 29). All these references are clearly intended to reflect the intense passions that percolate throughout the work, always on the verge of explosion or cataclysm. Lou Liberatore elaborates:

> The whole idea of fire and passion, flame and red, hot and burn is central to the play; it's about being fired up, the spark of Anna's heart, new passions being unleashed and so on. It's a very hot play![53]

Many other symbols occur throughout the play, not least in the references to Wagner's opera *The Flying Dutchman*. The Dutchman is condemned to perdition unless he can find a girl who will love him, but he is allowed only limited chances to succeed. He meets and falls in love with Senta, who is already in love with another; however, she does fall in love with the Dutchman and sacrifices herself for his sake, throwing herself into the fjord to save him from eternal damnation. Once she does so, "The sea starts boiling, the Dutchman's ship sinks, all hell breaks loose" (act 1, p. 15). The connections are obvious, the boiling sea being linked by Wilson to the stormy waters ahead for Pale and Anna.

Of the play's many symbols of awakening and liberation, two are perhaps the most potent: Anna's description of the live butterflies "beating their bodies against the walls" (act 1, p. 21) when she stayed at Robbie's family home during the funeral and of Pale unpinning them (act 1, p. 22). And later she wallows in metaphorical mud to acknowledge her potential fecundity after a bout with Pale: ". . . a brood sow. Flat out in the mud, with about ten piglets squealing around you, trying to nurse . . . . Their eyes rolled back in their heads? Lying back in the sun, in some other world" (act 2, pp. 57, 58).

Burn This is not a play capable of attracting a half-hearted response; critics and audiences either welcome it as a superbly vitriolic and observant study of art, life, and death in contemporary New York, or they condemn it as a worthless indulgence in sickly sentiment and pretentiousness. It has been variously described as "enthralling . . . an affecting humanist play,"[54] "a great play, part comedy and part tragedy,"[55] like "Chekhov on speed,"[56] "a fourhander *thirtysomething* . . . crossed with a wisecracking sitcom,"[57] "a wry Manhattan fantasy,"[58] and a "blazingly violent and hugely compelling story."[59]

The work certainly appears to inspire great affection in those who have been involved in its production. Each member of its London cast was delighted to have been associated with it, and the director believes that it is

a wonderful play . . . it's incredibly likable, incredibly moving, intelligent, just so rich and alive and full of perception and wit and humor and insight . . . Almost more than any play I have done, I can still watch this over and over and be moved by it and laugh at it.[60]

But *Burn This* has been castigated for what some see as sentimentality and implausibility of plot, as well as for its enormous dramatic reach, which has led at least one critic to observe that "Wilson has two or three plays occupying the same stage."[61] Others see it as "disappointingly flabby and soft-centered,"[62] as a work with "no centre of gravity and no centrifugal force"[63] and "a wishfulfilment exercise of the hoariest kind."[64]

I would argue that this play is far from sentimental, although the closing tableau could, for example, imply a "happy ending" in an insensitive production. In reality, Anna and Pale's predicament is far from cloying, or even optimistic: the couple recognize that what lies ahead, is inevitable and will almost certainly bring anguish and suffering:

Anna.   I don't want this . . . Oh, Lord, I didn't want this . . . .
Pale.   I know. I don't want it, either. I didn't expect nothin' like this.
   (act 2, p. 99)

Mel Gussow observes that Wilson "exposes deep, uncauterized emotional wounds—and offers no salve"[65] and that, while the play ends with Pale and Anna about to embark upon a perilous affair, "it would be precipitous to think of that as a happy ending. There is no guarantee of durability in this relationship."[66] The resignation with which they both confront the future is summed up by Wilson as

> something they both know they have to go through or they will never be able to look themselves in the face again. But the play is not about cottage small by the waterfall; it's not about moving to the suburbs and leading a normal life. I wouldn't give them a plugged nickel for their chances, but they wouldn't either, so who knows? It's not about that; it's not even about their *standards* by the end of the play. Having said that, I don't think they will destroy each other and I believe they will emerge as stronger people. What they feed on from each other is positive, not negative.[67]

It is true that a strong production is needed to convince an audience that this pair would eventually come together, after having been throughout as diametrically opposed as "two different breeds of animal in the zoo."[68] What is once again apparent throughout *Burn This* is Wilson's compassion for his characters. As Marshall Mason has stated, Wilson's "softness of heart"[69] often leads him into potentially sentimental situations, but he is constantly alert and on his guard to avoid them. I believe he has succeeded in so doing in this play, without in any way compromising or attenuating his affection for the characters.

Once again, critics are almost unanimous in their praise for Wilson's striking use of language, which is, as ever, meticulous and innovative, to match the massive scope of the work. Lasting three hours, *Burn This* is very demanding of its audience; as Lou Liberatore says, "There's a lot going on! . . . Some people hate it this long, others love it, most don't want it to end. There is *so* much."[70]

Pale's scrupulously constructed arias of frustration dominate the work, despite the fact that he is, for quite long periods, not even onstage. Their power is simply overwhelming, and his presence impossible to ignore. The audience's first encounter with this character sets the tone for the rest of the work: his initial, raging soliloquy against the world in general and against parking problems, city living, and potholes in particular embodies the primal scream of the disaffected—and furious—New Yorker whose need for instant gratification is thwarted by constant frustration:

> *Pale.* Goddamn this fuckin' place, how can anybody live this shit city? I'm not doin' it, I'm not drivin' my car this goddamn sewer, every fuckin' time. Who are these assholes? Some bug-eyed, fat-lipped half nigger, all right; some of my best friends, thinks he owns this fuckin' *space* . . . . Twenty-five fuckin' minutes I'm driving around this garbage street . . . . The only thing save this part of the city, they burn it down. . . . This has made me not as, you know—whatever—as I usually am. (act 1, pp. 25, 26)

Although threatening in the extreme, Pale invites audience identification with his plight. As Michael Coveney amusingly observes, "He hates everyone. You warm to him immediately."[71] Lou Liberatore believes Pale to be the very epitome of city life—brutal, impatient, and frustrated:

> Pale is very urban, of the city. He tells you what is on his mind absolutely. He doesn't edit. There is no pretense. Nothing at all . . . . The other characters don't talk about what they feel, they don't show what they feel, their emotions, but Pale does.[72]

Pale's relentless, corruscating obscenities almost collide as they explode from his lips. So keen is he to emphasize his disgust that he elides his sentences, as in "how can anybody live this shit city?" and "the only thing save this part of the city, they burn it down." There simply isn't time during this oratorio for syntactical niceties. Perhaps the most telling elision occurs in Pale's description of the individual who has initiated all of this wrath: "Some bug-eyed, fat-lipped half nigger, all right; some of my best friends, thinks he owns this fuckin' *space*." This callous invective reveals both viciousness and inherent racism before Pale quickly qualifies it by asserting, with a well-worn cliché, that he counts black people among his closest friends. The assertion is, however, difficult to take seriously in light of what has preceded it. A bit later, Pale is still worrying about the impression he has created, as he fumblingly states that the incident has confused and upset him: "This has made me not as, you know—whatever—as I usually am."

Another of Pale's seemingly wild and anarchic monologues occurs a little later in the play and illustrates even more vividly the creativity and depth of Wilson's linguistic invention. Again, Pale is angry with the world in general, but this time his bile is directed toward an irritating fellow-drinker in a downtown bar, as he describes the incident that has led to his hand being bloodied and bandaged:

> *Pale.* There was this character runnin' off at the mouth; I told him I'm gonna push his face in, he don't shut up. Now, this should be a fairly obvious statement, right? But this dipshit starts trying to explain to me what he's been saying *ad nauseam* all night, like there was some subtle gradation of thought that was gonna make it all right that he was mouthing this horseshit. So when I'm forced to bust the son of a bitch, he's down on the floor, he's dripping blood from a split lip, he's testing a loose tooth, and that fucker is *still talking*. Now, some people might think that this was the problem of this guy, he's got this motor going, he's not privy to where the shutoff valve is. But I gotta come to the conclusion that I'm weird. Cause I try to communicate with these jerkoffs in what is *essentially* the mother tongue, but no one is picking me up; they're not reading me. (act 1, p. 34)

Wilson's sparing, but effective, use of coarse language, together with the many abbreviated sentences and missing link words, exactly conveys the frustration and disbelief Pale feels. Barroom argot and naturalistic rhythms are manipulated and combined to create an impression of absolute authenticity. Pale's delivery of his tale in the present tense adds to the sense of spontaneity, and the sudden juxtaposition of elevated speech with raw obscenities simultaneously adds to the truth of the passage and lends it a poetic edge.

Wilson's character delineation is also first-rate. To analyze this one speech is to learn almost everything there is to know about Pale. The stylistic peculiarities that proliferate in this character's self-righteous, though ingenuous, speech patterns enable Wilson to convey his very essence. It is essential that Pale's unpredictability should be as fully realized as the many contradictions and juxtapositions that make up his personality. Wilson builds on these elements, giving them oral exposition that artfully depicts Pale's many incongruities.

That his violent, explosive tendencies can believably coexist with an almost refined sensibility is expressed by his use of sophisticated or subtle phrases such as "*ad nauseam*," "subtle gradation of thought" and "privy." These are not words one would expect to hear alongside the scatology and rushed phrasing that make up most of the speech.

Although holding down a conventional job as a restaurant manager and being married with children, Pale is aeons away from conformity; he is a complex mixture of violent thug and sensitive naif, and apparently has a predilection for alcoholic or chemical stimulation. (A little earlier he had admitted to Anna that he "did maybe a couple lines [of cocaine] with Ray" [act 1, p. 31], but claimed that it does not affect him.)

It is typical that he should shift the blame for his own violent actions to the victim; he stresses that he has been "forced to bust the son of a bitch." By refusing to take responsibility for his actions, he thereby exonerates himself. Even as his victim lies bleeding on the floor, Pale is unrepentant; instead, he maintains that, despite his very best efforts to make himself plainly understood, "in what is *essentially* the mother tongue," the idiot in question was incapable of comprehension. Believing himself superior to the "jerkoffs" he meets, Pale selflessly gives them every opportunity to communicate with him. That they seem unable to do so leads to his ironic observation that *he*, rather than they, must be "weird." This is clearly not meant to be taken at all seriously; by so denigrating himself, Pale makes it all the more plain for his audience that he is an all-too reasonable man who is constantly misunderstood and abused.

These excursions into the depths of Pale's angst are by no means mere excuses for scatalogical excess. Wilson manages to make them very funny by means of verbal juxtapositions. Pale constantly surprises us by the unexpected quaintness of a particular turn of phrase. Into the midst of his first ferocious outburst a grammatically strangled, yet almost polite, phrase is suddenly injected: "I mean no personal disparagement of the neighborhood in which you have your domicile, honey, but this street's dying of crotch rot" (act 1, p. 26).

Even this early on, Wilson hints at submerged, unseen elements of Pale's personality. This tirade may have the cadences of realistic speech, but it is far from prosaic. Its combination of high-flown phrases with the downright demotic is typical of Wilson, who frequently allows his wilder characters thus to expose unexpected sides.

It is instructive to compare Wilson's use of scabrous though emotionally loaded language with that used in similar situations in the drama of David Mamet. Mamet has, in fact, cited Wilson as a primary influence on his writing: "The contemporary playwright I admire the most is Lanford Wilson."[73] Conversely, Wilson greatly admires Mamet's work, calling him "a wonderful writer— I adore his plays."[74] Using similar linguistic techniques, Wilson structures and paces explosive tirades into muscular verse, the expletives taking on a resonance that elevates them above mere verisimilitude into a heightened dramatic idiom.

A good opportunity for comparison occurs in Mamet's *American Buffalo*. Teach, a weak, deluded small-time crook believes that his coconspirator Don has somehow betrayed him and has acted "unprofessionally" by siding with and supporting Bobby, his pathetic young drug-addicted friend. In fact, Don's protection of and love for Bobby is one of the few genuine demonstrations of emotion in the play. It is typical of Teach that he should misinterpret affection for treachery:

> *Teach.* You *fake.* You fucking *fake.* You fuck your friends. You *have* no friends. No *wonder* that you fuck this kid around . . . . You seek your friends with *junkies.* You're a joke on this street, you and him.[75]

Like Pale, Teach inverts or perverts facts in accord with his bitter self-righteousness; he instigates a (verbally) violent attack, blames others for it, and then demonstrates his convoluted sense of morality by his contemptuous and vicious denigration of his companions' friendship. There is great irony here, because Teach is conniving and perfidious in the extreme, easily capable of betraying a friend. The incongruity of the phrase, "You seek your friends with *junkies*," appears to escape him; he is, after all one of Don's friends, too. Mamet conveys Teach's spluttering anger with alliteration and the repeated use of expletives; here, the word "fuck" becomes merely one of many obscenities since, in this context, "fake" and even "friend" take on equally damaging connotations. Similarly, the alliterative impact of *"junkies"* and "joke" wields its own power.

In complete contrast to Pale's brutal—yet profoundly honest—outbursts, the other characters in *Burn This* do not really communicate. Lou Liberatore notes that "Anna is really unable to show her real feelings through language, except perhaps with Larry—when no-one else is in the room."[76] Rather than risk direct communication, Anna prefers on the whole to pepper her conversation with the kind of leaden clichés that can be found in pop songs, soap operas, and movies. Only occasionally is she aware that she is falling into a linguistic rut of the kind she would despise in others.

Having just returned from Robbie's funeral and, as a result, having been unable to exercise, she complains in tones reminiscent of soap opera that she is "completely out of touch with [her] body" (act 1, p. 19). Her reliance on pop psychology emerges when she observes that her sorrow is being wasted by not being sublimated into artistic expression: ". . . if I were still dancing, I'd probably be brilliant tonight" (act 1, p. 23).

Anna's essential shallowness of expression is thus analyzed by Juliet Stevenson:

> Some of the lines Anna has are desperate because they are so tinny . . . " a crackerjack feeler" for example! "I feel blue"! But of course that's partly what Wilson is writing about . . . She is just beginning to be aware of using second-rate, plagiarized song titles, instant accessible culture . . . the world of instant feeling which is very unresonant.[77]

Even Larry, by far the most articulate and witty of the characters onstage, relies on camp—verbally dexterous homosexual innuendo—to communicate. He hides his real feelings beneath a sardonic, self-deprecating humor and a barely suppressed yawn of hopeless resignation; instances of emotional exposure are rare and are quickly followed by a caustic dismissal.

The language of a successful and wealthy screenwriter of science-fiction blockbuster movies "reminiscent of something like *Total Recall*"[78] is no better. Burton's speech, often emotionally immature and contrived, shows little originality, although he is both confident and articulate. However, there are several moments when his speech breaks down. Speaking about his recent trip to Canada, he notes its influence on his writing style: "Amazing things happen to your mind, you feel like you're all alone, or you're one with the . . . something, or . . . well . . ." (act 1, p. 12).

The four characters' contrasting speech patterns afford a rich canvas for Wilson. Pale's vituperative animal ferocity, just occasionally hinting at a submerged finer sensibility; Anna's mostly second-hand yet heartfelt rambling; Larry's razor-sharp, though shallow, wisecracks; Burton's stolid phrasings—all enable the playwright to capture with wit and verisimilitude the conversational styles of contemporary New York.

Burn This is another Wilson play that includes characters whose sexuality is either ambiguous or blatantly noncomformist. Although containing only one openly homosexual character, Larry, the play features people who, while appearing strongly heterosexual, exhibit personality traits at variance with their chosen projected image. The ostensibly macho Pale, for example, has a strongly feminine side in conflict with the urban aggressor he presents to the world.

The homoerotic aura pervading the work continues with Burton, who constantly, though good-humoredly, rebuffs Larry's joky sexual advances and suggestive innuendo. Burton is drawn as a "man's man": athletic, self-sufficient, and teaching akido at the local YMCA. A well-heeled screenwriter of blockbuster movies, he appears a man in control of his destiny. But one night he temporarily doffs his usual sophisticated, man-about-town image to candidly recall a homosexual episode from his youth when he was fellated in the snow by a passing stranger. As Michael Simkins observes, however, much of Burton's speech is contrived:

> He's very fond of what are, in effect, slightly forced anecdotes. He loves to talk about himself and his experiences . . . and likes to impress upon his audience that "I've lived as well."[79]

His happy memory of the incident is thus a little too self-conscious, a little too pat: "It was very nice, and I never thought about it. And it didn't mean anything, but I've never been sorry it happened or any of that crap" (act 2, p. 63). This is not to suggest that Burton may harbor suppressed homosexual longings.

More likely, he just wishes to demonstrate to his friends his broad-minded and enlightened attitude.

However, his choice of reminiscence to illustrate these traits is an interesting one. Notwithstanding his "acceptance" of Larry, subtle suggestions exist (not least in his strident, overcompensatory telling of the above anecdote) that Burton may nourish homophobic fears. In spite of his assertions to the contrary, he is perhaps homophobic—the only true homophobe in the play.

Pale may project a superficial homophobia, but it is not borne out in his relationship with Larry. Indeed, the pair share the most domestic scene in the whole play, and, although dismissive of Larry's camp persona, Pale seems able to communicate with him. John Malkovich believes that Pale is not so much homophobic as contemptuous of the New York superficial glitziness and sophisticated swagger so often projected by the likes of Larry. He believes that the play is a veiled comment on the inherent snobbery of New York:

It [New York] is full of quite selfish, mindless, narcissistic bullies and it drives me berserk . . . . I can just land there and after a few minutes I'm enraged.[80]

About Pale's contemptuous attitude to Larry, he observes:

What he doesn't like is that Larry is a little too witty and needs to be punched . . . . there is an almost exquisitely painful provincialism about people who come from the cities as though they were somehow terribly cultured and artistic, which they rarely are . . . those who live there are supposed to be so *cool* . . . they think they are so interesting and superior. This goes for the criminal element, the media element, and the sort of *Village Voice* element or whatever. For a character like Pale, this sort of thing is just a target.[81]

By the end, each character has learned something of value. Anna has grown both as an artist and as an individual; having tasted the extremes of experience, she is enriched and, probably, less prone to easy reliance on compromise and concession. In Anna's new-found maturity, Pale has found a match for his ardor and strength of feeling; for the first time, he experiences love and enters a relationship built on genuine emotion rather than on empty sentiment. And possibly, within the confines of a supportive relationship, his own creative impulses can be set free; perhaps his "artistic temperament" can now be channelled into positive and fulfilling directions.

Larry is finally forced to acknowledge the futility and barrenness of his chosen lifestyle; living vicariously through the love affairs of others is deeply unsatisfactory. However, his part in helping Pale and Anna to come together could signal a change for the better; observing the inevitability of their relationship—despite its many problems—might impel him to seek out a partner, even though aware that such a step could be potentially hazardous.

In losing Anna to Pale, Burton has learned that, for her, his attractiveness has been based largely on convenience. He is forced to recognize his limitations and that he and Anna were and never could be a suitable match. What beguiles Anna about Pale is his complete lack of phoniness and pretension—two prominent components of Burton's personality.

Burn This spreads its dramatic reach wide with an ambition, humor, and inventive use of language that place it very firmly at the forefront of Wilson's dramatic canon. Far from being "a wish fulfillment exercise of the hoariest kind,"[82] it is one of his most important and vibrant works into which he has incorporated many themes examined in previous plays, but all the while extending them to new depths.

Conclusion

Because of the breadth of time over which Lanford Wilson's three major urban plays were written, they constitute a neat summation of his achievements as a dramatist. From the earliest risk-taking and experimentation that dominate *Balm in Gilead*, through the almost complete *volte face* of the largely traditional and lyrical *The Hotl Baltimore* and, finally, to the versatile linguistic maturity of *Burn This*, Wilson has proven himself a challenging and adaptable playwright whose works change to suit the mood and express the idiom of the times.

In addition to utilizing every aspect of Wilson's exceptional ear for the poetic potential of everyday language, his urban plays span three very different decades. The works are so much products of their own contemporary time-frame that they are almost iconic; the daily rituals of their characters reflect the essence of what it was to live in such a place at such a time. Wilson truly does seem to possess the knack of portraying the linguistic *zeitgeist* of a given era.

Thus, the psychedelic nuances of the counterculture of the 1960s combine with the slang of the streets to provide a shocking, though illuminating, glimpse into a drug-fueled ghetto rarely imagined, let alone dramatized. Similarly, the sad realization of the 1970s that the previous decade's promise of optimism and joyous liberalism were but a short-lived phenomenon permeates the "hip" yet disconsolate badinage of *The Hotl Baltimore*'s residents. And, finally, the self-conscious and brittle shallowness of much of the chatter of the supposedly self-confident late 1980s Manhattanites in *Burn This* proclaims the disappointed spirit of the age. The "boom" time of that decade was, in Wilson's eyes, a phenomenon of much noise and little substance that ultimately led to a depersonalization of society and a subsequent breakdown in human communication. In that time, a tarnished veneer of jejeune sophistication emerged, which masked much emotional retardation and a general feeling of dissatisfaction. That his characters continue to proclaim their fundamental optimism is testimony to their resilience and refusal to be beaten down by circumstance.

What persists throughout the whole of Wilson's drama, both rural and urban, is a fundamental humanity and compassion for those he dramatizes. For this playwright, *every* individual is worthwhile; *every* character, irrespective of social standing, faults, or inadequacies, is equally worthy of attention. Each has their own story to tell, and Wilson tells it without recourse to any moralistic judgment. He clearly loves mankind and enjoys writing about *people*. That his characters seem so real, so recognizable is no accident, so deeply are they based in his own life experiences and in the experiences of those he has known.

To understand this aspect of Wilson's work is to comprehend his aim as a dramatist. He has stated that his main objective is to portray as accurately as possible the times in which he lives and to show humanity in all of its diversity without apology. One can, therefore, understand how his constant strivings after authenticity in language, after the truth of any given situation, and after honesty in portrayal cohere with his goal. Since each of his plays achieves these standards to such a large degree, Wilson can be said to have succeeded in his stated aims, and the three urban plays discussed here are perhaps the most perfect realization to date of his chosen ambitions.

Notes

Chapter 1. *From Missouri to Manhattan*

1. Guy Flately, "Lanford is One 'L' of a Playwright," *New York Times*, 22 April 1973, p. 21.
2. Tanya Berezin, interview with author, 18 September 1991, Circle Repertory Company, New York.
3. Mel Gussow, *"Talley's Folly*: A Valentine Hit—Lanford Wilson on Broadway," *Horizon*, May 1980, pp. 30–36.
4. Don Shewey, "I Hear America Talking," *Rolling Stone*, 22 July 1982, p. 18.
5. Ibid.
6. Trish Dace, "Plainsongs and Fancies," *Soho Weekly News*, 5 November 1980, p. 3.
7. Lanford Wilson, cited in *Dictionary of Literary Biography: Twentieth Century American Dramatists*, vol. 7, (Detroit: Gale Research Co., 1981) p. 352.
8. Gussow, *"Talley's Folly*: A Valentine Hit," p. 33.
9. Ibid.
10. Wilson, cited in *Dictionary of Literary Biography*, p. 353.
11. Ibid.
12. Michael Smith, *Village Voice*, cited in *Dictionary of Literary Biography*, p. 355.
13. Michiko Kakutani, "I Write the World As I See It Around Me," *New York Times*, 8 July 1984, pp. 4, 6.
14. Wilson, cited in *Dictionary of Literary Biography*, p. 358.
15. Richard L. Coe, *Washington Post*, cited in *Dictionary of Literary Biography*, p. 350.
16. Wilson, interview with Barnet Kellman, cited in *Dictionary of Literary Biography*, p. 359.
17. John J. O'Connor, "The Wilson Touch, *Wall Street Journal*, 22 May 1970, reprinted in *New York Theatre Critics' Reviews*, October 1970, p. 208.
18. Clive Barnes, "Immediacy Illuminates Wilson's *Lemon Sky*," *New York Times*, 18 May 1970, reprinted in *New York Theatre Critics' Reviews*, 12 October 1970, pp. 208–9.
19. Wilson, cited in *Dictionary of Literary Biography*, p. 362.
20. Berezin, interview with author, 18 September 1991, Circle Repertory Company, New York.
21. Ibid.
22. Ibid.
23. Ibid.
24. Ibid.
25. Ibid.
26. *Dictionary of Literary Biography*, p. 360.
27. Berezin, interview with author, 18 September 1991, Circle Repertory Company, New York.

28. Lou Liberatore, interview with author, 27 September 1990, Shaftesbury Avenue, London.

29. Wilson, cited in *Dictionary of Literary Biography*, p. 360.

30. Harold Clurman, "Theatre," *The Nation*, 5 March 1973, pp. 313–14.

31. Ibid.

32. Peter Buckley, "Circle Repertory Theater," *Horizon*, May 1980, p. 37.

33. Berezin, interview with author, 18 September 1991, Circle Repertory Company, New York.

34. Leslie Bennetts, "Marshall Mason Explores a New Stage," *New York Times*, 11 October 1987, p. 3.

35. Buckley, "Circle Repertory Theater," p. 37.

36. Jennifer Allen, "Portrait: Lanford Wilson," *Life*, June 1980, p. 30.

37. Frank Rich, "*Angels Fall*: Lanford Wilson's Apocalypse," *New York Times*, 18 October 1982, p. C15.

38. Jane Edwardes, "Beyond the Pale," *Time Out*, 23–30 May 1990, pp. 14, 15.

Chapter 2. *Concerns, Poetry, and Dramatized Experience*

1. Berezin, interview with author, 18 September 1991, Circle Repertory Company, New York.

2. Martin J. Jacobi, "The Comic Vision of Lanford Wilson," *Studies in the Literary Imagination*, no. 2, 21 (Fall 1988): 121.

3. Gussow, "*Talley's Folly*: A Valentine Hit," p. 32.

4. Berezin, interview with author, 18 September 1991, Circle Repertory Company, New York.

5. Samuel Freedman, "Lanford Wilson Enjoys a Triumph over Time," *New York Times*, 26 December 1985, p. C13.

6. Allen, "Portrait: Lanford Wilson," pp. 29–30.

7. Robert Berkvist, "Lanford Wilson—Can He Score on Broadway?," *New York Times*, 17 February 1980, pp. 1, 3.

8. Lanford Wilson, interview with author, 14 September 1991, Circle Repertory Company, New York.

9. Gussow, "*Talley's Folly*: A Valentine Hit," p. 36.

10. Kakutani, "I Write the World As I See It Around Me," pp. 4, 6.

11. Ibid.

12. Ibid.

13. Wilson, interview with author, 14 September 1991, Circle Repertory Company, New York.

14. Marshall Mason, interview with author, 15 September 1991, New York.

15. Wilson, interview with author, 14 September 1991, Circle Repertory Company, New York.

16. Lanford Wilson, *The Rimers of Eldritch* (New York: Farrar, Straus and Giroux, 1967 (Noonday Press edition, 1988), p. 3.

17. Lanford Wilson, *The Madness of Lady Bright*, in *The Rimers of Eldritch & Other Plays* (New York: Farrar, Straus and Giroux, 1967 (Noonday Press edition, 1988), p. 75.

18. Ibid.

19. Wilson, interview with author, 14 September 1991, Circle Repertory Company, New York.

20. Gussow, "*Talley's Folly*: A Valentine Hit," p. 32.

21. Friedrich Hebbel, cited in *Playwrights on Playwriting*, ed. Toby Cole (New York: Hill & Wang, 1982), p. 286.

22. Wilson, interview with author, 14 September 1991, Circle Repertory Company, New York.

23. Allen, "Portrait: Lanford Wilson," p. 30.

24. Wilson, interview with author, 14 September 1991, Circle Repertory Company, New York.

25. Mason, interview with author, 15 September 1991, New York.

26. Ibid.

27. Berezin, interview with author, 18 September 1991, Circle Repertory Company, New York.

28. Liberatore, interview with author, 27 September 1990, Shaftesbury Avenue, London.

29. Wilfrid Sheed, "The Stage," *Commonweal*, 29 April 1966, p. 82.

30. Edith Oliver, "The Theatre: Off Broadway," *The New Yorker*, 2 April 1966, p. 124.

31. Edith Oliver, "The Theatre: Off Broadway," *The New Yorker*, 31 March 1973, p. 77.

32. Gerald Weales, "American Theater Watch 1979–1980," *Georgia Review* 34 (1980): 498.

33. Ibid.

34. Wilson, interview with author, 14 September 1991, Circle Repertory Company, New York.

35. Mason, interview with author, 15 September 1991, New York.

36. Henry Schvey, "Images of the Past in the Plays of Lanford Wilson," in *Essays on Contemporary American Drama*, ed. Hedwig Bock and Albert Wertheim (Munich: Max Huebler Verlag, 1981), pp. 225–40.

37. Ibid.

38. Mason, interview with author, 15 September 1991, New York.

39. Berezin, interview with author, 18 September 1991, Circle Repertory Company, New York.

40. Ibid.

41. Edith Oliver, "The Theatre: Off Broadway," *The New Yorker*, 8 May 1978 p. 90.

42. Harold Clurman, *The Nation*, 5 March 1973, p. 314.

43. Emile Zola, cited in *Playwrights on Playwriting*, p. 12.

44. Wilson, interview with author, 14 September 1991, Circle Repertory Company, New York.

45. Shewey, "I Hear America Talking," p. 18.

46. John Simon, "Playing with Fire," *New York Magazine*, 13 February 1984, pp. 68–69.

47. John Simon, "Likable but Unlikely Transplant," *New York Magazine*, 15 May 1978, pp. 77–78.

48. Wilson, interview with author, 14 September 1991, Circle Repertory Company, New York.

49. Shewey, "I Hear America Talking," p. 20.

50. O'Connor, "The Wilson Touch," p. 208.

51. Martin Gottfried, *A Theater Divided: the Postwar American Stage* (Little, Brown & Co., 1967) pp. 300–301.

52. Liberatore, interview with author, 27 September 1990, Shaftesbury Avenue, London.

53. Mason, interview with author, 15 September 1991, New York.

54. Hebbel, *Playwrights on Playwriting*, p. 288.

55. Wilson, interview with author, 14 September 1991, Circle Repertory Company, New York.

56. Ibid.

57. Wilson, cited in *Dictionary of Literary Biography*, p. 363.

58. Liberatore, interview with author, 27 September 1990, Shaftesbury Avenue, London.

59. Shewey, "I Hear America Talking," p. 20.

60. Ibid.

61. *Washington Post*, 26 September 1968, p. D23.

62. Michael Simkins, interview with author, 19 November 1990, Stoke Newington, London.

63. Kakutani, "I Write the World As I See It Around Me," pp. 4, 6.

64. Eleanor Blau, "How Lanford Wilson Writes with Actors in Mind," *New York Times*, 27 January 1983, p. C15.

65. Berezin, interview with author, 18 September 1991, Circle Repertory Company, New York.

66. Wilson, interview with author, 14 September 1991, Circle Repertory Company, New York.

67. Michael Warren Powell, interview with author, 14 September 1991, Circle Repertory Company, New York.

68. Wilson, interview with author, 14 September 1991, Circle Repertory Company, New York.

69. Shewey, "I Hear America Talking," p. 20.

70. Wilson, interview with author, 14 September 1991, Circle Repertory Company, New York.

71. Gussow, "*Talley's Folly*: A Valentine Hit," p. 36.

72. Kakutani, "I Write the World As I See It Around Me," pp. 4, 6.

73. Wilson, interview with author, 14 September 1991, Circle Repertory Company, New York.

74. Thornton Wilder, *Our Town*, (New York: Samuel French, 1965), p. 36.

75. Walter Kerr, "The Hazards and Pains Plaguing an Actor's Life," *New York Times*, 3 February 1983, p. C15.

76. Gerald Weales, "*Angels Fall*, Epistle of Peter to New Mexico," *Commonweal*, 17 December 1982, pp. 690–91.

77. Gottfried, *A Theater Divided: The Postwar American Stage*, pp. 300–301.

78. Mason, interview with author, 15 September 1991, New York.

79. Clive Barnes, "Wilson's Tale Told Brilliantly," *New York Post*, 12 June 1981, reprinted in *New York Theatre Critics Reviews*, 7–13 September, 1981, p. 185.

Chapter 3. *Balm in Gilead*

1. Lanford Wilson, *Balm in Gilead and Other Plays*, (New York: Farrar, Strauss, and Giroux, 1965 (Noonday Press edition, 1988), p. 3.

2. John Beaufort, "Definitive Revival of Lanford Wilson's First Full-Length Play," *The Christian Science Monitor*, 18 June 1984, p. 22.

3. Gene Barnett, *Lanford Wilson*, quoted in *Contemporary Authors Bibliographical Series—American Dramatists*, vol. 3 (Detroit: Gale Research Co., 1989), p. 443.

4. Robert Brustein, "Post-Naturalist Triumph," *New Republic*, 5 November 1984 pp. 27–29.

5. Beaufort, "Definitive Revival of Lanford Wilson's First Full-Length Play," p. 22.

6. Wilson, interview with author, 14 September 1991, Circle Repertory Company, New York.

7. Shewey, "I Hear America Talking," p. 20.

8. Wilson, interview with author, 14 September 1991, Circle Repertory Company, New York.

9. Ibid.

10. Ibid.

11. Ibid.

12. Powell, interview with author, 14 September 1991, Circle Repertory Company, New York.

13. Ibid.

14. Wilson, interview with author, 14 September 1991, Circle Repertory Company, New York.

15. Ibid.

16. Ibid.

17. Kakutani, "I Write the World As I See It Around Me," pp. 4, 6.

18. Ibid.

19. Ibid.

20. Wilson, interview with author, 14 September 1991, Circle Repertory Company, New York.

21. Ibid.

22. Ibid.

23. Wilson, *Balm in Gilead*, p. 3.

24. Wilson, *Balm in Gilead*, p. 68.

25. Ibid.

26. Ibid.

27. Ibid, p. 3.

28. Ibid, p. 9.

29. Ibid, p. 33.

30. Ibid, p. 10.

31. Leslie Bennetts, "Marshall Mason Explores a New Stage," *New York Times*, 11 October 1987, p. 7.

32. Mason, interview with author, 15 September 1991, New York,

33. Wilson, interview with author, 14 September, 1991, Circle Repertory Company, New York.

34. John Malkovich, interview with author, 27 September 1990, Lyric Theatre, London.

35. Ibid.

36. Wilson, *Balm in Gilead*, p. 5.

37. Ibid, p. 4.

38. Ibid, p. 26.

39. Ibid, p. 7.

40. Ibid, p. 7.

41. Ibid, p. 20.

42. Ibid, p. 41.

43. Ibid, p. 57.

44. Ibid, p. 71.

45. Kakutani, "I Write the World As I See It Around Me," pp. 4, 6.

46. Gen. 37:25 and Jer. 8:22.

47. Hos. 12:11 and 68.

48. 1 Samuel 13:7.
49. Beaufort, "Definitive Revival of Lanford Wilson's First Full-Length Play," p. 22.
50. Margaret Atwood, *The Handmaid's Tale*, (London: Virago Press, 1987), p. 314.

Chapter 4. *The Hotl Baltimore*

1. Gussow, *"Talley's Folly*: A Valentine Hit," p. 34
2. Lanford Wilson, *The Hotl Baltimore* (New York: Dramatists Play Service, 1973), p. 7.
3. Berkvist, "Lanford Wilson—Can He Score on Broadway?" pp. 1, 3.
4. Kakutani, "I Write the World As I See It Around Me," pp. 4, 6.
5. Richard Watts, "The Hotel That Was Dying" *New York Post*, 23 March 1973, reprinted in *New York Theatre Critics Reviews*, 19 April 1973, p. 307.
6. Jack Kroll, "Grand Hotel," *Newsweek*, 26 February 1973, p. 91.
7. Wilson, interview with author, 14 September 1991, Circle Repertory Company, New York.
8. Harold Branam, "Lanford Wilson," in *Critical Survey of Drama*, vol. 5, ed. Frank N. Magill, (Englewood Cliffs, N.J.: Salem, 1985), pp. 2095–2103.
9. Ibid.
10. Wilson, *The Hotl Baltimore*, p. 7.
11. Mel Gussow, "The Unwanted People of *Hotl Baltimore*," *New York Times*, 8 February 1973, p. 37.
12. Wilson, *The Hotl Baltimore*, p. 32.
13. Ibid.
14. Ibid, p. 33.
15. Mason, interview with author, 15 September 1991, New York.
16. Gussow, *"Talley's Folly*: A Valentine Hit," p. 34.
17. Kroll, "Grand Hotel," p. 91.
18. Gussow, "The Unwanted People of *Hotl Baltimore*," p. 37.
19. Oliver, "The Theatre Off Broadway," p. 77.
20. Ibid.
21. Clurman, "Theatre," p. 314.
22. Flately, "Lanford Is One 'L' of a Playwright," p. 21.
23. Wilson, interview with author, 14 September 1991, Circle Repertory Company, New York.
24. Flately, "Lanford Is One 'L' of a Playwright," p. 21.
25. John Simon, "Folie à deux," *New York Magazine*, 21 May 1979, pp. 76–78.
26. Ann Crawford Dreher, in *Dictionary of Literary Biography*, p. 362.
27. Berkvist, "Lanford Wilson—Can He Score on Broadway?" pp. 1, 3.
28. Wilson, *The Hotl Baltimore*, p. 7.
29. Mason, interview with author, 14 September 1991, New York.
30. Flately, "Lanford Is One 'L' of a Playwright," p. 21.
31. Gene A. Barnett, "Recreating the Magic: An Interview with Lanford Wilson," *Ball State University Forum* 25; (Spring, 1984); 57–74.
32. Wilson, interview with author, 14 September 1991, Circle Repertory Company, New York.
33. Kakutani, "I Write the World As I See It Around Me," pp. 4, 6.
34. Wilson, *The Hotl Baltimore*, p. 7.

35. Mason, interview with author, 15 September 1991, New York.
36. Wilson, *The Hotl Baltimore*, p. 5.
37. T. S. Eliot, "East Coker," *The Four Quartets* (London: Faber & Faber, 1979), pp. 26, 27.

Chapter 5. *Burn This*

1. Robert Allan Ackerman, interview with author, 3 October 1990, Lyric Theatre, London.
2. Liberatore, interview with author, 27 September 1990, Shaftesbury Avenue, London.
3. Mason, interview with author, 15 September 1991, New York.
4. Wilson, interview with author, 14 September 1991, Circle Repertory Company, New York.
5. Jack Kroll, *Newsweek*, cited on back cover of Lanford Wilson, *Burn This* (New York: Farrar, Straus and Giroux, 1987, Noonday Press edition, 1988).
6. Malkovich, interview with author, 27 September 1990, Lyric Theatre, London.
7. Wilson, interview with author, 14 September 1991, Circle Repertory Company, New York.
8. Mason, interview with author, 15 September 1991, New York.
9. Wilson, interview with author, 14 September 1991, Circle Repertory Company, New York.
10. Malkovich, interview with author, 27 September 1990, Lyric Theatre, London.
11. Mason, interview with author, 15 September 1991, New York.
12. Bennetts, "Marshall Mason Explores a New Stage," p. 3.
13. Ibid.
14. Ackerman, interview with author, 3 October 1990, Lyric Theatre, London.
15. Wilson, interview with author, 14 September 1991, Circle Repertory Company, New York.
16. Berezin, interview with author, 18 September 1991, Circle Repertory Company, New York.
17. Wilson, interview with author, 14 September 1991, Circle Repertory Company, New York.
18. "John Malkovich," *Omnibus*, BBC2 Television, 7 September 1990.
19. Ibid.
20. Ibid.
21. Ibid.
22. Ibid.
23. Milton Shulman, "Dangerous Liaison," *Evening Standard*, 30 May 1990, p. 39.
24. Jack Tinker, "High Wire Magic with No Holds Barred," *Daily Mail*, 30 May 1990, reprinted in *London Theatre Record*, vol. 10, 21 May–3 June 1990, p. 716.
25. Ackerman, interview with author, 3 October 1990, Lyric Theatre, London.
26. Simkins, interview with author, 19 November 1990, Stoke Newington, London.
27. *Omnibus*, 7 September 1990.
28. Kenneth Hurren, "Theatre," *The Mail on Sunday*, 3 June 1990, reprinted in *London Theatre Record*, p. 715.

29. Irving Wardle, "Shattered Sanctuaries," *The Independent on Sunday*, 3 June 1990, reprinted in *London Theatre Record*, p. 723.

30. Michael Billington, "A Sweeter Shade of Pale," *The Guardian*, 30 May 1990, reprinted in *London Theatre Record*, p. 717.

31. Berezin, interview with author, 18 September 1991, Circle Repertory Company, New York.

32. Mason, interview with author, 15 September 1991, New York.

33. Ackerman, interview with author, 3 October 1990, Lyric Theatre, London.

34. Liberatore, interview with author, 27 September 1990, Shaftesbury Avenue, London.

35. Ibid.

36. Juliet Stevenson, interview with author, 1 November 1990, Queen's Park, London.

37. Wilson, interview with author, 14 September 1991, Circle Repertory Company, New York.

38. Malkovich, interview with author, 27 September 1990, Lyric Theatre, London.

39. Mason, interview with author, 15 September 1991, New York.

40. Ibid.

41. Ackerman, interview with author, 3 October 1990, Lyric Theatre, London.

42. Stevenson, interview with author, 1 November 1990, Queen's Park, London.

43. Ibid.

44. Ackerman, interview with author, 3 October 1990, Lyric Theatre, London.

45. Stevenson, interview with author, 1 November 1990, Queen's Park, London.

46. Malkovich, interview with author, 27 September 1990, Lyric Theatre, London.

47. Ibid.

48. Ibid.

49. Simkins, interview with author, 19 November 1990, Stoke Newington, London.

50. Malkovich, interview with author, 27 September 1990, Lyric Theatre, London.

51. Liberatore, interview with author, 27 September 1990, Shaftesbury Avenue, London.

52. Stevenson, interview with author, 1 November 1990, Queen's Park, London.

53. Liberatore, interview with author, 27 September 1990, Shaftesbury Avenue, London.

54. Billington, "A Sweeter Shade of Pale," p. 717.

55. Thomas M. Disch, "Theater," *Nation*, 15 November 1987, pp. 569–70.

56. Charles Osborne, "Like Chekhov on Speed," *The Daily Telegraph*, 31 May 1990, reprinted in *London Theatre Review*, p. 723.

57. Paul Taylor, "Creative Blocks," *The Independent*, 31 May 1990, p. 12.

58. Maureen Paton, *"Burn This," The Daily Express*, 4 June 1990.

59. Sheridan Morley, *Herald Tribune*, 6 June 1990, reprinted in *London Theatre Review*, p. 715.

60. Ackerman, interview with author, 3 October 1990, Lyric Theatre, London.

61. Rhoda Koenig, *Punch*, 8 June 1990, reprinted in *London Theatre Review*, p. 716.

62. Martin Hoyle, *Financial Times*, 30 May 1990, reprinted in *London Theatre Review*, p. 717.

63. Clive Hirschorn, *The Sunday Express*, 3 June 1990, reprinted in *London Theatre Review*, p. 717.

64. Jim Hiley, *The Listener*, 7 June 1990, p. 32.

65. Mel Gussow, "Lanford Wilson's Lonely World of Displaced Persons," *New York Times*, 15 October 1987, p. 5.

66. Ibid.

67. Wilson, interview with author, 14 September 1991, Circle Repertory Company, New York.

68. Stevenson, interview with author, 1 November 1990, Queen's Park, London.

69. Mason, interview with author, 15 September 1991, New York.

70. Liberatore, interview with author, 27 September 1990, Shaftesbury Avenue, London.

71. Michael Coveney, "Burn These Wigs," *The Observer*, 5 June 1990, p. 58.

72. Liberatore, interview with author, 27 September 1990, Shaftesbury Avenue, London.

73. Gussow, *"Talley's Folly*: A Valentine Hit," p. 36.

74. Wilson, interview with author, 14 September 1991, Circle Repertory Company, New York.

75. David Mamet, *American Buffalo*, (London: Methuen, 1978), p. 104.

76. Liberatore, interview with author, 27 September 1990, Shaftesbury Avenue, London.

77. Stevenson, interview with author, 1 November 1990, Queen's Park, London.

78. Liberatore, interview with author, 27 September 1990, Shaftesbury Avenue, London.

79. Simkins, interview with author, 19 November 1990, Stoke Newington, London.

80. Edwardes, "Beyond the Pale," p. 15.

81. Malkovich, interview with author, 27 September 1990, Lyric Theatre, London.

82. Hiley, *The Listener*, p. 32.

Bibliography

Works by Lanford Wilson

Angels Fall. New York: Farrar, Straus and Giroux, 1983 (Noonday Press edition, 1990).

Balm in Gilead and Other Plays. New York: Farrar, Straus and Giroux, 1965 (Noonday Press edition, 1988).

Burn This. New York: Farrar, Straus and Giroux, 1987 (Noonday Press edition, 1988).

Days Ahead. In *The Rimers of Eldritch & Other Plays.* New York: Farrar, Straus and Giroux, 1967 (Noonday Press edition, 1988).

Fifth of July. New York: Hill and Wang (Noonday Press), 1978.

The Great Nebula in Orion and Three Other Plays. New York: Dramatists Play Service, 1973.

Home Free! In *Balm in Gilead and Other Plays.* New York: Farrar, Straus and Giroux, 1965 (Noonday Press edition, 1988).

The Hotl Baltimore. New York: Dramatists Play Service, 1973.

The Madness of Lady Bright. In *The Rimers of Eldritch & Other Plays.* New York: Farrar, Straus and Giroux, 1967 (Noonday Press edition, 1988).

The Rimers of Eldritch & Other Plays. New York: Farrar, Straus and Giroux, 1967 (Noonday Press edition, 1988).

The Sand Castle and Three Other Plays. New York: Dramatists Play Service, 1970.

Serenading Louie. New York: Hill & Wang, 1970.

Stoop. In *The Sand Castle and Three Other Plays.* New York: Dramatists Play Service, 1970.

This Is the Rill Speaking. In *The Rimers of Eldritch & Other Plays.* New York: Farrar, Straus and Giroux, 1967 (Noonday Press edition, 1988).

Secondary Sources and Suggested Other Reading

Busby, Mark. *Lanford Wilson.* Boise, Idaho: Boise State University Press, 1987.

Chekhov, Anton. *Chekhov: The Major Plays.* Translated by Ann Dunnigan. New York: New American Library, 1964.

Clurman, Harold. *The Fervent Years: The Group Theatre and the 30s.* New York: Da Capo Press, 1975.

Cole, Toby, ed. *Playwrights on Playwriting.* New York: Hill & Wang, 1982.

Contemporary Literary Criticism, Vols. 7, 14, and 36. Detroit: Gale Research Co., 1977, 1980, and 1986.

Dreher, Ann Crawford. *Lanford Wilson* in *Dictionary of Literary Biography: Twentieth Century American Dramatists* vol. 7, part 2, K–Z. Edited by John MacNicholas. Detroit: Gale Research Co., 1981.

Eliot, T. S. *Four Quartets*. London: Faber & Faber, 1944.

Gorky, Maxim. *The Lower Depths*. In *Five Plays*. London: Methuen, 1988.

Inge, William. *Bus Stop*. New York: Dramatists Play Service, 1955.

Jacobi, Martin J. *Lanford Wilson* in *Contemporary Authors—Bibliographical Series: American Dramatists*, vol. 3. Detroit: Gale Research Co., 1989. See also vols. 17–20.

Mamet, David. *American Buffalo*. London: Methuen, 1978.

Thomas, Dylan. *Under Milk Wood*. London: J. M. Dent & Sons, 1958.

Wilder, Thornton. *Our Town*. New York: Samuel French, 1965.

Williams, Tennessee. *Sweet Bird of Youth, A Streetcar Named Desire, and The Glass Menagerie*. Harmondsworth. Middlesex: Penguin Books, 1985.

Index

Ackerman, Robert Allan, 95, 98, 101, 103, 106–7, 108, 113
Albee, Edward, 19
Altman, Robert, 51
American Buffalo (Mamet), 118–19
American Theatre Project, 19, 22
Anderson, Sherwood, 59
Angels Fall (Wilson), 28, 40, 43, 54–55, 56, 59, 78, 97
Angels in America (Kushner), 41
Atwood, Margaret, 78

Balm in Gilead (Wilson), 15, 17, 19, 22, 31, 32, 40, 42, 44, 45, 47, 51, 52, 56, 57, 58, 59, 60, 61–79, 80, 81, 83, 85, 96, 97, 98, 123
Behan, Brendan, 68
Bent (Sherman), 41
Berezin, Tanya, 19, 22–23, 24, 25, 30, 32, 41, 46, 54–55, 99, 102–3
Bertolucci, Bernardo, 101–2
Betrothal, A (Wilson), 28
Blue Velvet (Lynch), 33
Brontosaurus (Wilson), 27, 42–43, 56, 77–78
Burn This (Wilson), 28–29, 31–32, 40, 41–42, 44, 53, 54, 55, 56, 94–122, 123
Bus Stop (Inge), 58, 59

Caffe Cino, 18, 19, 20, 21, 22
Cather, Willa, 59
Cat on a Hot Tin Roof (Williams), 57
Chekhov, Anton, 45, 53, 59, 60, 113; *The Cherry Orchard*, 60; *The Three Sisters*, 59, 60; *Uncle Vanya*, 59, 60
Cherry Orchard, The (Chekhov), 60
Cino, Joseph, 18, 19, 20, 21
Circle Repertory Company, 19, 22–28, 29, 52, 53
Circle Repertory Theatre, 19, 24, 26, 27

Clurman, Harold, 24–25, 47
cummings, e.e., 22–23

Days Ahead (Wilson), 19, 49
Death in Venice (Mann), 41
Death of a Salesman (Miller), 16
Dickens, Charles, 57

Edward II (Marlowe), 41
Eliot, T. S., 93

Family Continues, The (Wilson), 27
Fierstein, Harvey, 41
Fifth of July, The (Wilson), 27, 40, 42, 44, 49–50, 81
Flying Dutchman, The, 112
Foster, Paul, 18
Four Quartets, The (Eliot), 93

Gingham Dog, The (Wilson), 20–21
Glass Managerie, The (Williams), 16, 58
Gorki, Maxim, 62, 66
Great Nebula in Orion, The (Wilson), 26, 56
Group Theatre, The, 24, 53
Guare, John, 18

Handmaid's Tale, The (Atwood), 78
Hebbel, Friedrich, 39, 52
Him (e.e. cummings), 22–23
Hoiby, Lee, 26
Home Free! (Wilson), 18, 19, 22, 36, 42, 97
Hostage, The (Littlewood), 58, 66
Hot l Baltimore, The (Wilson), 17, 27, 28, 31, 32, 37–38, 40, 42, 43, 45, 52, 57, 59, 60, 80–93, 97, 123
Hour Glass, The (Wilson), 17
Hughes, Barnard, 54
Hurt, William, 25

Iceman Cometh, The (O'Neill), 45, 66
Ikke, Ikke, Nye, Nye, Nye (Wilson), 26–27

137

In Circles (Stein), 66
Inge, William, 57, 58, 59
Ionesco, Eugene, 18, 34

Kushner, Tony, 41

La Mama Experimental Theatre Club, 18, 19, 20, 22
Lemon Sky (Wilson), 16, 20, 21, 40, 57
Lesson, The (Ionesco), 18
Liberatore, Lou, 24, 41, 51–52, 53, 54, 95, 103–4, 111, 112, 114, 115, 119
Littlewood, Joan, 58, 66
Lower Depths, The (Gorki), 62, 66
Ludlow Fair (Wilson), 19
Lynch, David, 33

Madness of Lady Bright, The (Wilson), 19, 22, 36–37, 40, 41, 43, 48–49, 60, 81, 97
Mahoney, John, 100
Malkovich, John, 19, 28, 55, 66, 70–71, 96, 97, 100, 101, 102, 105, 109, 111, 121
Mamet, David, 39, 79, 118
Marlowe, Christopher, 41
Mason, Marshall, 19, 21, 22, 23, 25, 27, 28, 35, 40, 44, 46, 48, 52, 59–60, 64, 85, 89, 92, 95, 97, 98, 103, 106, 114
Meisner, Sanford, 24
Metcalf, Laurie, 100
Millay, Edna St. Vincent, 50
Miller, Arthur, 16, 50
Miss Williams: A Turn (Wilson), 19
Mound Builders, The (Wilson), 27, 46, 54, 56
Murdoch, Iris, 99

New York Shakespeare Festival, 17–18, 26
Night of the Iguana (Williams), 83
No Trespassing (Wilson), 18

Odets, Clifford, 24, 53
O'Neill, Eugene, 17, 45, 66
Our Town (Wilder), 58, 59

Papp, Joseph, 26
Playwright's Laboratory, 29
Powell, Michael Warren, 22, 55, 64

Rabe, David, 18
Redwood Curtain (Wilson), 29, 40, 60
Reeve, Christopher, 53
Rimers of Eldritch, The (Wilson), 19, 22, 30, 33, 36, 37, 38, 85
Rosencrantz and Guildenstern are Dead (Stoppard), 45

Sand Castle, The (Wilson), 19, 58
Serenading Louie (Wilson), 26, 39, 48, 56
Severed Head, A (Murdoch), 99
Sex Is Between Two People (Wilson), 19
Sextet (Yes) (Wilson), 26
Shepard, Sam, 18, 39, 79, 100
Sherman, Martin, 41
Simkins, Michael, 54, 101, 110, 120
So Long at the Fair (Wilson), 18
Stein, Gertrude, 66
Steppenwolf Theatre Co., 19, 28, 100
Stevenson, Juliet, 104, 107, 108, 111, 114, 119
Stewart, Ellen, 18, 19
Stoop (Wilson), 26, 36
Stoppard, Tom, 45
Streetcar Named Desire, A (Williams), 57, 102
Summer and Smoke (Hoiby), 26

Tale Told, A (Wilson), 27–28
Talley and Son (Wilson), 28
Talley's Folly (Wilson), 27
"Talley" plays (Wilson), 32, 97
Tarkington, Booth, 59
Thirkield, Rob, 19, 22
This Is the Rill Speaking (Wilson), 19, 22, 30, 36, 51, 59
Thomas, Dylan, 69
Three Sisters, The (Chekhov), 59, 60
Thymus Vulgaris (Wilson), 28
Torch Song Trilogy (Fierstein), 41
Twin Peaks (Lynch), 33

Uncle Vanya (Chekhov), 59, 60
Under Milk Wood (Thomas), 69
Untitled Play (Wilson), 20

Wandering: A Turn (Wilson), 19
"War in Lebanon" Trilogy (Wilson), 27
Wilder, Thornton, 57, 58, 59
Williams, Tennessee, 16, 17, 26, 56, 57;

Cat on a Hot Tin Roof, 57; *The Glass Menagerie,* 16, 58; *A Streetcar Named Desire,* 57, 102; *Night of the Iguana,* 83
Wilson, Lanford, 15, 16, 17, 38, 20, 21, 24, 26, 32, 33, 34, 35, 37, 39, 43–44, 47, 50, 51, 52, 54, 55, 56, 57, 63, 64–65, 66–67, 70, 75, 78, 80, 81, 82, 85, 88, 89, 90, 95–96, 97, 99, 105, 114, 118; *Angels Fall,* 28, 40, 43, 54–55, 56, 59, 78, 97; *Balm in Gilead,* 15, 17, 19, 22, 31, 32, 40, 42, 44, 45, 47, 51, 52, 56, 57, 58, 59, 60, 61–79, 80, 81, 83, 85, 96, 97, 98, 123; *A Betrothal,* 28; *Brontosaurus,* 27, 42–43, 56, 77–78; *Burn This,* 28–29, 31–32, 40, 41–42, 44, 53, 54, 55, 56, 94–122, 123; *Days Ahead,* 19, 49; *The Family Continues,* 27; *The Fifth of July,* 27, 40, 42, 44, 49–50, 81; *The Gingham Dog,* 20–21; *The Great Nebula in Orion,* 26, 56; *Home Free!,* 18, 19, 22, 36, 42, 97; *The Hot l Baltimore,* 17, 27, 28, 31, 32, 37–38, 40, 42, 43, 45, 52, 57, 59, 60, 80–93, 97, 123; *The Hour Glass,* 17; *Ikke, Ikke, Nye, Nye, Nye,* 26–27; *Lemon Sky,* 16, 20, 21, 40, 57; *Ludlow Fair,* 19; *The Madness of Lady Bright,* 19, 22, 36–37, 40, 41, 43, 48–49, 60, 81, 97; *Miss Williams: A Turn,* 19; *The Mound Builders,* 27, 46, 54, 56; *No Trespassing,* 18; *Redwood Curtain,* 29, 40, 60; *The Rimers of Eldritch,* 19, 22, 30, 33, 36, 37, 38, 85; *The Sand Castle,* 19, 58; *Serenading Louie,* 26, 39, 48, 56; *Sex Is Between Two People,* 19; *Sextet (Yes),* 26; *So Long at the Fair,* 18; *Stoop,* 26, 36; *A Tale Told,* 27–28; *Talley and Son,* 28; *Talley Folly,* 27; *This Is the Rill Speaking,* 19, 22, 30, 36, 51, 59; *Thymus Vulgaris,* 28; *Untitled Play,* 20; *Wandering: A Turn,* 19

Yeats, W. B., 84

Zola, Emile, 47